A

Big

New

Free

Happy

Unusual

Life

Self-Expression
and
Spiritual Practice
for
Those
Who
Have
Time
for
Neither

BROADWAY BOOKS / NEW YORK

A
Big
New
Free
Happy
Unusual
Life

NINA WISE

Broadway Books titles may be purchased for business or promotional use or for special sales. For information, please write to: Special Markets Department, Random House, Inc., 1540 Broadway, New York, NY 10036.

Excerpt from "Silence and Dancing," *Alive Together, New and Selected Poems*, by Lisel Mueller, Louisiana State University Press, Baton Rouge and London, 1996. Reprinted by permission from the publisher.

"Remember," from *In the Direction of the Divine/*Poems, forthcoming; used with permission of the author, originally published in Goodman Artworks Catalogue, 1975, used with permission of the publisher

PRINTED IN THE UNITED STATES OF AMERICA

BROADWAY BOOKS and its logo, a letter B bisected on the diagonal, are trademarks of Broadway Books, a division of Random House, Inc.

Visit our website at www.broadwaybooks.com

Library of Congress Cataloging-in-Publication Data

Wise, Nina, 1948–
    A big new free happy unusual life: self-expression and spiritual practice for those who have time for neither / Nina Wise.—1st ed.
        p. cm.
    1. Creative ability—Problems, exercises, etc. 2. Creative thinking—Problems, exercises, etc. I. Title.

BF408 .W57 2002
153.3'5—dc21   2001049965

FIRST EDITION

Designed by Caroline Cunningham

ISBN 0-7679-1007-9

10 9 8 7 6 5 4

This book is dedicated to my mother, who was fired from teaching elementary school when she insisted that drumming was as important as learning arithmetic; and to my father, who passed away before the book was bound, yet from the great beyond continues to radiate his enthusiastic support.

The title of this book is borrowed from Grace Paley's short story "Goodbye and Good Luck" (*The Collected Stories*). A suitor is asking the protagonist for her hand. He says, "Rosie, I offer you a big new free happy unusual life."

I have been deeply inspired by Grace Paley over the years—by her wit, her intelligence, her wordsmithing, and the depth of her heart revealed on the page.

Many years ago, I received a card, a photograph of a woman jumping. When I decided to write this book, I knew immediately that I wanted to use that photograph for the jacket. I found the photographer, Peter Groat, who told me that the jumping woman was his wife, Jenny Hunter Groat. Jenny, it turns out, studied and performed improvisational dance in the fifties and sixties, and is now a painter and a devoted meditator. What I had recognized in the photograph was a kindred spirit, a woman who decades before me was already pioneering the path I ended up following and writing about here, in these pages, which she so graciously adorns.

Contents

Foreword

Sometimes in your life, you meet a person who just makes you laugh, whose infectious spirit makes you want to get up and dance. For me, this person is Nina Wise. Nina brings a remarkable aliveness to her creative work and to this book. And she invites you, the reader, to join her in opening up to the same depth of joy and creativity in your own life.

I've been told the story of a six-year-old girl who asked her mother where she was going one afternoon. The mother replied that she was headed for the university to teach her students how to draw and paint. "You mean they've forgotten?" her daughter asked, amazed. Many of us have forgotten how to give voice to our creativity. And yet it is said that play—our ability to let go, dance, sing, create—is one of the most wondrous expressions of our aliveness. We enjoy seeing raccoons, otters, monkeys, and children share this happiness. Without nurturing, the vitality of our own body and spirit can dry up. The poet John Ciardi explains "an ulcer is an unkissed imagination taking its revenge for having been jilted. It is an undanced dance, an unpainted watercolor, an unwritten poem."

In Zen there is a term called beginner's mind, a state of nonjudgmental awareness, of open-mindedness and spontaneity. As you follow the pages of this book, Nina offers a hundred ways to enter the state of beginner's mind as you spark, reclaim, and enliven your true creative abandon. "Okay," she says, "I'll be first," and you see her talking prim New York editors into closing their eyes and hand dancing in their thirty-third floor offices. Now it's your turn.

Belt out a song to the sky, sing in your car, or croon an old love song, skat, ska, and slide. Go to the beach and build driftwood sculptures. Dance as if no one is watching. Run, jump, circle, fall. Leave creative messages on your answering machine, paint wild art in secret, have costume parties, depression parties, play games in bed.

Nina reminds us that even our spiritual or religious side can become too serious, a grim duty. So chant, build altars, sing in hospitals even to those who are dying. Cultures like those of India and Bali, or the carnivals of Rio and Venice, remind us how to combine sacred ritual with wild and chaotic beauty. Let the arts flower on every street corner, in every office and school, as the blessings of the gods.

Wake up. Let your life blossom. And let Nina's invitation remind you to laugh, to play, to trust yourself and the creative spirit that abides within you.

May you be happy.

Jack Kornfield
Spirit Rock Meditation Center
Woodacre, California
December 2001

A Note from the Author

I am writing this note on November 2, 2001, six weeks after the destruction of the World Trade Center towers, which caused the death of thousands of people, including hundreds of firefighters who perished in their heroic efforts to save lives. To date, a hospital worker, two United States postal workers, and a journalist have died from inhaled anthrax and several others have been hospitalized with the disease. Reports of hundreds of civilian casualties of the bombing in Afghanistan are beginning to trickle across the airwaves, along with accounts of hundreds of thousands of refugees facing a harsh winter without food or shelter.

The aftershocks of these tragedies befalling ordinary people caught up in unordinary circumstances roll over the country and the world in ever-widening waves of grief, fear, rage, and a grave disappointment in the state of human evolution at the beginning of the twenty-first century. Many of us ponder our personal and collective fate and wonder what we can do as individuals, communities, and societies to participate in the creation of a safe world for ourselves and future generations.

To heal the world, Zen monk Thich Nhat Hanh tells us, we must begin by healing ourselves. He tells the story about boat people fleeing Vietnam who fell prey to wild seas and acts of dehumanizing violence by pirates. If only one person on the boat was able to remain calm and peaceful, the likelihood of survival for all of the passengers was greatly enhanced. We might think of the planet as one of those fragile boats, afloat in a sea that is now stricken with violence. If each of us develops the capacity for equanimity, kindness, and compassion, the likelihood that we will survive as a species and create the kind of world we wish to leave for our children and for their children is exponentially increased.

While our government is urging us to shop 'til we drop as an expression of our love for our country, most of us understand in our hearts that democracy is not, and has never been, about consumerism. Democracy is about freedom. And freedom is alive and well within us no matter how infrequently we visit the mall. Our longing for freedom cannot be satisfied by cars or houses or diamonds; by private jets or offshore bank accounts or caviar; by miniature computers or mighty weapons. Our longing for freedom can only be satisfied by recognizing that we are each sufficient as we are, and that what feeds us has nothing to do with what we buy and everything to do with an inherent vitality of soul.

Creative self-expression, a time-honored methodology for accessing our spiritual natures, for making contact and giving form to our subconscious, for establishing interpersonal bonds and building community, and for enhancing vitality, is essential to our welfare personally and collectively. We can, together, take this moment in human history to wake up to who we already know ourselves to be: a free people dedicated to a sane and just world made up of individuals who celebrate their common humanity and this planet of indescribable beauty through song and dance, poetry, and care for all sentient beings.

Introduction

I have been performing and teaching improvisation since 1972. Over the decades, I have asked my students what brings them to my workshops and they have reported a singular motive: No matter how satisfying their love relationships, how successful their careers, how remarkable their children, or how voluminous their wealth, they have felt that something was missing in their lives. Many have taken up spiritual practices to address this longing, and while these practices have proved to be effective in cultivating insight and peace of mind, the practitioners have continued to feel an unnamed hunger. I have come to understand that this gnawing in the heart is a longing to rekindle daily life with the spirit of self-expression, spontaneity, and play.

Sometimes when I meditate, I experience an inner glow, a feeling of inherent well-being that seems unassailable. And so I dust off my pillow and stand up, ready to engage in activity. Ten minutes, or an hour, or two hours later, I find myself in a state of frustration or anger or depression—the workload is too heavy, the traffic is too thick, the state of the world is too malevolent, the time is too short—and my well-being has slipped away, somehow beyond my grasp, ephemeral despite my earlier experience of the steady state of this subliminal underground current of equanimity. I long to find the avenue back, or down, or in, that will lead me to that inner knowing of radiant being that is not dependent in any way on outer circumstances.

What I provide here are the access routes I have discovered that are expressive in nature—the activities of song, and dance, and poetry, and visual art that have the potential to transform our lives.

You already know everything you need to know to live a big, free, happy, unusual, enthusiastic, and amusing life. Creativity is an inborn aspect of being alive. All you need to do is relax and let it out. And if you do, you will find yourself, without the slightest hint of effort, dancing in your living room, singing in the car, writing poetry on cocktail napkins, and noting the dinner plate is a perfect canvas for a painting made of food.

The
Art
of
Freedom

Remembering Who We Are

"We all want to be free. That is human nature. We want to be
free from pain and suffering and limitations. If we look deeply
into our hearts, we know what we want; we are in love with the
condition of liberation. Our pain is the feeling of alienation or
separation from our Beloved, which is this freedom. . . . But
finding true nature is not for the timid. It requires courage and
a sense of adventure, a fearless heart, and optimistic strength."
— HAMEED ALI

The Art of Freedom

It is our nature to be free and it is our nature to express that freedom, spontaneously and without hesitation, through song, and dance, and painting, and poetry, and prayer. In the same way that the universe gives birth to uncountable shapes, forms, colors, and beings in a grand panoply of flowing, changing manifestation, we, too, are of the nature to give birth to myriad forms of expression. In the same way that birds sing, and lions roar, and prairie dogs dance, and cicadas chant, and water sculpts rock, and sunsets paint the sky, we, too, are of the nature to sing, and roar, and dance, and chant, and sculpt, and paint. And we are also of the nature to pray—to give thanks and reverence to this Creation that we are an inextricable part of as witnesses and participants.

All of us are free, and this freedom is our very essence; we need not do anything at all to achieve it. But distracted by the stories we tell ourselves about our lives and who we believe ourselves to be within these stories, we forget that our essential nature is unencumbered and liberated. Instead, we enforce stringent rules on ourselves and each other, confining our freedom of self-expression to meager slots of time in rigidly defined arenas. Dancing on the sidewalk is forbidden except in the movies. Singing while riding your bicycle is forbidden unless absolutely no one is within earshot. Spontaneously talking in a French accent because your lover has just left you and you're a little depressed and feel like being someone else for a minute—forbidden. And we, ourselves, are the prison guards who keep ourselves incarcerated. So it is we, ourselves, who must open the doors and step out into the light and gaze unflinchingly at the boundless sky which is reflecting our own nature.

Freedom does not mean that we cease to feel pain, but that we have the courage to move through the depths of suffering and the pinnacles of joy alike. And as we allow ourselves to express whatever arises, fully and without judgment, we discover that what ails us transforms into what heals us, and the distinction between pain and delight fades—this is the alchemy of creative self-expression.

It is our nature to be free, but we forget, since it is also our nature to forget. Spiritual practice is a method of remembering who we are. And spiritual practice need not be restricted to sitting still and watching the breath. As Rumi says, "There are many ways to kneel and kiss the ground."

Reclaiming What We Have Lost

"If you don't change the direction in which you are going, you will end up where you are headed."

CONFUCIUS (reputedly)

We speak of progress. We speak of evolution. We imagine we are moving forward, fast. But where are we going? If we look at the evidence, we recognize that as we have progressed technologically, we have systematically divested ourselves of a vital source of well-being.

Since the inception of the human species and until only decades ago, daily life was infused with art making. We crafted our own tools, we sewed our own clothing, we built our own shelters, we cultivated our own food. We sang songs that we made up, songs that were passed down to us, and songs that were given to us by the gods. We danced together matching our steps to the steps of our companions. We built musical instruments out of hides and sinew, twine and bent wood. We painted on walls and on our bodies and our implements. These creative acts enhanced our well-being as individuals, strengthened family bonds, knit communities together, and provided access to states of being that invoked insight and wisdom. We as a species cannot reside in psychological and physical health if we abandon the very activities that maintain well-being.

Everyone is creative. Creativity is our very nature. But for many of us, the creative impulse has gone into hiding. "I can't draw, I can't sing, I can't dance," we confess to each other, and we plant ourselves in front of the television for the evening. But the creative impulse that is at the core of all being remains robust within us.

Creativity is about having the courage to invent our lives—to concoct lovemaking games, cook up a new recipe, paint a kitchen cabinet, build sculptures on the beach, and sing in the shower. Creativity is about our capacity to experience the core of our being and the full range of our humanness.

The question of how to become more creative is not about *learning* anything, or even *doing* anything, but about allowing whatever arises to gain expression. To do this, we must bypass the voice inside of us that says stop. The censoring mind is clever and has an entire litany of reasons we must refrain from expressing ourselves: *You are a bad dancer so sit back and watch while the skillful ones dance. And you certainly can't paint so don't even try because you will embarrass yourself. You sing off-key and you can't hold a rhythm—you will disturb everyone within earshot if you open your mouth. And if you happen to disregard this sage advice, you will make a total fool of yourself and no one will ever love you or give you a job.* We obey this voice as if being guided by inner wisdom; but when we tune in, we hear a quieter voice calling out to us to express ourselves freely. This is the voice that can liberate us. If we listen and respond, our lives become rich with the pleasure creative freedom provides.

Many years ago, I learned an important lesson about the value of self-expression. I was ending a long-term relationship and spent day after day sequestered in my studio where I played a particularly sad love song over and over again as I rolled slowly across the dance floor letting the tears flow. After a week of crying and floor rolling, my heartache lifted. I was surprised by a wave of disappointment—I actually missed the romantic pain that had moved me effortlessly around the room. As I emerged from the swoon of grief, I realized that inherent in the act of art making was a relief from pain—suffering became more bearable when expressed through art.

"Art is a wound turned into light," the French painter Georges Braques wrote. Worked with as material, the very feelings and incidents that cause our suffering can be transformed through our creative acts into sources of amusement or a bittersweet pleasure. While drawing or painting, singing or dancing, writing poetry or prose, rearranging the furniture or arranging flowers, we allow our psyche a way of emerging from the dark recesses of the mind into the perceived realm of form. In the same manner that our bodies are able to heal from cuts and bruises and colds, our hearts are able to heal from emotional injuries if we find a means for healthy expression. And this expression does not necessarily require that we spend hours of time in our studios—creative expression can occur in minutes, anywhere.

I spent a remarkable afternoon with a friend recently. As we walked near his office along a mesa toward the beach, my friend asked me about my work and I told him I was writing this book. He paused for a moment and admitted in a somewhat confessional tone that the one element in his life that he feels is missing is spontaneous play. He is internationally successful, committed to his marriage and his meditation practice, but he doesn't play.

As we continued our walk, my friend asked if I would teach him one of the movement practices and I described *A Moment of Movement* to him. He stood close to me on a rise of white sand, and with the sky and the ocean as his backdrop, began to dance. I fully delighted in the intimate pleasure of observing his arms sweep from side to side, his back curve and arch, his knees dip, and when he finished, I applauded with genuine enthusiasm. My friend then asked me to move so that he could observe. I stood yards away and closed my eyes. I had been feeling sad due to a conflict that had arisen with a professional colleague that morning so I let the melancholy move me. My head dropped to my chest, my shoulders caved downward, my knees drooped until I fell, and I rolled slowly across the sand. When I finished, I felt lighter, and I relished the moment of release and truthfulness.

"I get it," my friend said, grinning.

By witnessing my movement, he had come to understand what I had been attempting to say with language—that when a person dances, we see not only physical movement but also the inner life of the person who is moving. And by being the mover who is watched, we allow what is inside our hearts and bodies to come out, and we feel better.

My friend and I continued our walk, appreciating the touch of sand against our bare feet, the sudden emergence of the sun from a bank of low clouds. Our conversation flowed with a notable ease, quickened by our having danced for each other. When the time came for us to return, I asked my friend if he would do an experiment with me.

"What is it?" he asked.

"Take one minute and build a sculpture out of things you find," I said.

"One minute?" he asked.

"Okay, two," I said.

He leapt up and ran to a huge plastic buoy that had washed up on the beach. I stayed where I was, sorting white pebbles from shale. When we were done, we looked at each other's art. My friend had assembled a coil of ocean-drenched rope, propped on top of the buoy by a piece of driftwood, and at the foot of the sculpture he had set the bright orange shell and turquoise claw of a crab.

There is a word in Sanskrit I learned from an article in a music magazine (and have now unfortunately forgotten), that means the way the psyche is affected when looking at art. I have since been told that there are many Sanskrit words describing specific influences that regarding an artwork has on the mind. But in English there are no such words so we are vague about how we are affected by our gaze. Yet we feel the transformation. And we are affected not only by looking at art but also by making art.

Walking back to our cars, my friend and I paused for a moment at the top of the mesa and, looking out over the rolling waves, we confessed to each other how happy we were to have played together.

The practices we had done were easy—games that anyone can play—and took only a few minutes each. Yet the effect was profound in ways that can be spoken and ways that cannot be spoken. The games we played were not particularly unique; we have all at one time or another danced for a minute and arranged objects in a way that has pleased us. But most of us do not spend our afternoons this way, even if we are with a friend whom we love and trust and are on the beach and the sun is shining and shells and pebbles and driftwood abound.

The reclamation of our creative spirits is an easy and enjoyable journey. We only need to devote a modicum of courage and short, but regular, periods of time to find our way back to our essential nature, which is unfettered, playful, and free. The heart of most spiritual teachings is the same: that each person is born in a state of perfection, and this quality is innate to being itself and does not require that we do anything at all to achieve it. But due to personal, family, intergenerational, and cultural conditioning we lose sight of our innate wholeness, and we look to the world of things to satisfy our longing. Yet our longing can only be satisfied by turning our gaze within and becoming aware of who we truly are: radiant beings, already wise, already rich, already content. We know this, but we forget. All we need do to remember who we are is to reconnect with the freedom within our hearts, which is always there, waiting for us to come home.

> "In the greatest confusion there is still an open channel to the soul. It may be difficult to find because by mid-life it is overgrown . . . But the channel is always there, and it is our business to keep it open, to have access to the deepest part of ourselves."
>
> SAUL BELLOW

Guidelines

You may decide to read this book and follow all the practices as you go chapter by chapter. If followed in this order, you will notice that the practices build one upon another so that you feel guided step-by-step through a process that unfolds and spirals.

You may read the book through and do only a few of the practices, or none of them at all, and then later when you feel the need, pull the book from the shelf the way you reach for a cookbook and turn to the section to which you are drawn. You will find that each section can stand alone.

You may read the book through ignoring the practices altogether and suddenly find yourself dancing in the living room, or singing while you walk the dog. The notions encoded in these pages can influence the mind whether you do the recommended practices or not, but you will benefit most if you engage in some form of creative self-expression on a regular basis. You might invent your own practices, or amend the ones presented here to suit your own taste.

You may pick up the book when you have an evening alone, or when you are going on a weekend getaway with a friend. You might close your eyes, flip through the pages, and land somewhere, guided by chance.

You might choose to set aside "studio time" and take an hour or two a week to do a combination of practices: movement, voice, writing, and visual.

You might want to only spend a minute, here and there, doing one or another of the practices.

Feel free to use the book in the way that best suits you; create your own style.

To assist you in whatever manner you choose, I offer the following guidelines, which apply throughout.

1. Begin each practice from stillness and take a moment to empty the mind of thought. Then see what comes. Instead of planning what you will write or sing or draw before doing it, improvise. If you decide what to do before acting, you limit the possibility of what can arise in the moment of action. Pay attention to what you've done, but don't anticipate what you will do next. In this way, you live in the present moment.

2. Be true to whatever you are feeling physically. If you are tired, work in a tired way. Experiment with minimal movement—fold a finger or roll on the

floor. Hum the quietest of melodies. Draw a single line. Trying to be energetic when you are exhausted is a lie and creative self-expression is fundamentally about delivering the truth.

On the other hand, if you are feeling frenzied and lively, move with vigor, sing with vigor, write vigorously. This is what is authentic.

3. Respond to *emotional* impulses as they arise moment to moment. If you are feeling irritated or resistant, move or sing or draw or write in a way that expresses irritation or resistance. If you are frightened, express fear. This doesn't mean that if you are angry you stomp your feet and wave your fists in the air, or if you are sad that you pout and fold your arms over your chest or draw a face with a frown. These are clichés and *demonstrate* feeling rather than *express* feeling. Instead, feel the energy that anger produces and allow that energy to move the body as you dance, to move the hand as you paint or write. You might jump up and down pointing your index fingers into the air. You might write quickly in big black letters scrawled across the page. You might throw paint at a paper spread out across the floor. If you are sad, feel the energy that sadness produces and let it move you. You might quiver and jiggle your elbows. You might let paint drip like tears onto paper. You might describe the sensation of tightness in your chest.

4. Include everything. If you fall unexpectedly, go with it. If you want to bounce off the walls, bounce off the walls. If you are hot, be hot. If a siren interrupts your song, sing with the siren. We often try to push reality aside, thinking that whatever is occurring in our lives at the moment should be different from what is actually happening. In this work, what is arising moment to moment is the source of our movement, sound, images, and speech, is the source of our material. Push nothing aside. Even the impulse to repress a physical impulse, or an emotion, or an image can become our material.

We can talk ourselves out of creative expression because we find the environment we are in not conducive to such expression. But in truth, we can create anywhere, anytime. We can sing in an elevator, dance in bed, draw on the pavement. Include everything.

5. Surrender. Let go of believing that you are in charge of the way your life goes, the way your work goes, the way you move or sing or draw or write

poetry. Give up, yield, lose control. There is a creative impulse in us that is better at art making than our conscious minds. "Our senses, our instincts, our imagination are always a step ahead of our reason," writes Octavio Paz. Surrender to the subconscious. Let go.

6. Surprise yourself. Go for what you don't know, what you've never done before. When you are moving in a way that is off balance, quirky, odd, awkward, you are doing good work. When your hand is moving on the page as you write more quickly than your mind is working, you are accessing the subconscious, contacting flow. When you find yourself working in ways that are unfamiliar and uncomfortable, feed more energy into the process. Go as far as you can into that new territory.

7. Take risks physically and emotionally. Not to the extent that you injure yourself or your partners, but to the extent that you move beyond what is known into what is unknown. Risk adds excitement and interest to your work. It is fine to take a risk and to fail. You might attempt balancing on the tips of your toes as you list sideways, lose your balance, and fall. The fall is as dramatic as the balance. You might try writing about an event in your life you have difficulty articulating and then experience difficulty articulating it. Great! Move to the edge of what your capacity is, expand your ability, and continue to move to the next edge. Like life, art making is not a static event occurring in safe space, but a dynamic unfolding of new possibilities. Challenge yourself to move beyond physical and emotional comfort.

8. Make mistakes. Be stupid, awkward, ridiculous. Write the worst poem imaginable. Paint a horrible picture. Sing out of tune. Embarrass yourself. Often our attempts to be good or skillful camouflage a deeper part of ourselves. When we let ourselves make mistakes, we discover the wisdom inherent in our stupidity, the grace embedded in awkwardness, the truth couched in the ridiculous. When you fail in your efforts, congratulate yourself for your courage and vitality.

9. Commit to what you are doing. Commitment plus energy equals enjoyment. Don't hold back. Feed energy into your action. The censoring mind will be chanting its mantra, *This is boring, you're making a fool of yourself, this is*

the worst piece of rubbish, you are wasting valuable time. Let the censor roll, it's out of your control anyway, but don't pay too much attention. Commit to what you are doing with the gift of energy. You don't have to believe in what you are doing, you simply have to do it.

When you look carefully at the elements of the list above, you will notice that they are linked. In reality, commitment is not separate from risk taking, surprise is not separate from surrender, including everything is not separate from responding to emotional and physical impulses. All of these guidelines point to a single action, which is in its essential nature, indescribable. Guidelines can only point you in a direction, they cannot take you there.

One of my teachers, the great Advaita master H. W. L. Poonja, often used the following metaphor when talking about his own teaching. He said that his guidance was like a finger pointing at the moon. If you get riveted on staring at the teacher's finger, he admonished, you will never see the moon. A teacher cannot touch the moon, or bring it out of the sky to place it in the palm of your hand. He can only point, and if you follow his finger, and continue out into the night sky, then you will see the moon.

Effort, No Effort, and Love

One morning, after spending several hours writing about how energy without effort is the key to unlocking the door to creative freedom, I took a break and decided to go to the bike store because I needed a lock and helmet. I thought about biking to the bike store, which is only blocks from my house, but the weather was unseasonably sweltering and I also needed to go to the nursery. After twenty minutes of thinking—*Drive . . . no bike . . . it's way too hot to pedal . . . yet I don't want to waste resources . . . how will I carry the plants? . . . you'll figure it out and you need the exercise . . . you can exercise later*—I grabbed my keys and took off in the car.

A young woman with spiky black hair, wearing khaki pants rolled up at the cuff, fitted the helmet to my head and adjusted the straps with an expert's touch. Because she seemed kind and like someone who probably had given her car away to a nonprofit and now biked everywhere, I confessed to her that I wasn't confident I would actually ever ride the shiny new bicycle that was now parked and ready on my patio, confessed that I might never find it convenient or have the inclination.

"It isn't a question of convenience or inclination," she said. "It's a question of force. You have to force yourself at first, then you get accustomed to it and you ride all the time."

I realized she was right. Until you get used to it, you have to force yourself—you have to make up your mind to ride that bicycle, and just do it. It's the same with making life art; you have to force yourself at first. You have to make up your mind to get up for a minute and dance, or burst into song in the car, or write poetry on a used envelope, or draw designs on frosty windowpanes. And then you fall in love with the whole experience and don't have to force yourself anymore. Then it's a question of love.

two

Something in the Way We Move

Rediscovering the Body

O, but they danced, did they ever;
she danced like a devil, she'll tell you,
recalling a dress the color of sunrise,
hair fluffed to sea-foam,
some man's, some boy's
damp hand on her back
under the music's sweet, hot assault

and wildness erupting inside her
like a suppressed language,
insisting on speaking itself
through her eloquent body,

a far cry
from the well-groomed words on her lips.

—LISEL MUELLER

Freedom Is Contagious

When I was eighteen, I bought a backpack and headed for Europe. After a few weeks of shivering in the rain-drenched north, I followed the call of winter sun and made my way to Crete where I took up residence in a cliffside cave above a beach of pale sand. In the evenings, I dined with fellow travelers in a café that served mounds of humus and platefuls of olives and cold slices of salt-cured cucumber. The local men, with dark skin and thick mustaches and black hair, sat around the tables smoking unfiltered cigarettes and drinking ouzo. As the night wore on, the men started to sing, and then, with their arms wrapped around each other's shoulders, they danced. Sweat glistened on their foreheads as they dipped their knees and kicked their legs, and a deep laughter rolled out of their bellies. Beckoning and calling out, they were not satisfied until all of us—black-clad widows, fiancées with red lipstick, cooks in stained aprons, long-haired hippies, barefoot toddlers—were up on our feet and dancing.

We did not speak the same language, but words did not matter; words meant nothing. What mattered was that we were dancing together, stomping to the beat together, sweating and smelling bad together, catching each other's eyes and seeing there the knowing of dancing, the pleasure of dancing, hair mussed, clothes wet, lipstick faded, cheeks glowing, together, dancing.

What I experienced in Crete while dancing with strangers was a crystalline happiness that had little to do with eminence, fortune, or romance but had everything to do with the eminent fortune of falling in love with life. What I experienced in Crete while dancing with strangers had nothing to do with religion but had everything to do with making life holy.

If we are to fully know freedom, we must find that freedom not only in the mind but also in the body, the house of our being. The physical body is our medium for connecting the sacred and the profane, the transcendent and the ordinary, a medium for giving expression to our essential nature, which is un-encumbered and open and zesty. When we develop the capacity to express ourselves spontaneously through movement, we experience liberation as a *felt* reality—and as we come to know this feeling of freedom in the body, as we taste it and savor the taste, we begin to express ourselves more and more freely. And this liberation is very personal but not at all a private affair; this liberation in us is sensed by everyone with whom we come into contact and is infectious.

Humans respond viscerally to movement. As we watch a dancer undulate or a deer bound, a gymnast soar or an ice skater spin, our sympathetic nervous systems fire neurons to sinew, muscle and bone so that we are literally *feeling* the movement that we are *seeing*. The work of learning to move with the grace that is latent within us as human beings is of benefit not only to ourselves, but is also of benefit to the people we meet, who pick up that ease for a moment in their own bodies—freedom calling out to itself and answering.

The Buddha taught several methods to achieve enlightenment. One was to "feel the body in the body," to focus awareness on felt experience. While this instruction sounds remarkably simple, most of us are unable to center our attention on physical sensations. Instead, we are distracted by our thoughts and emotions and pay little notice to how our bodies are feeling unless we are in severe pain or in the throes of primal pleasure. As we become ensconced in work at our desks, or hypnotized in front of the television, as we stand in line at the grocery store or sit in airports waiting for a plane, we become numb to the needs of the body and we ignore the impulse to move: to stretch the arms, roll the shoulders, rotate the ankles, and lengthen the spine. And we have deadened ourselves so repeatedly that many of us are no longer aware of the feelings in the body, even though sensations are coursing throughout our waking hours.

On the way home from a performance festival in Italy one summer, I had a long layover at JFK. The many hours of traveling in a cramped airplane had aggravated an old dance injury, so I sat down cross-legged on the gray carpet of the waiting area and proceeded to move through a series of stretches. In the late seventies, yoga had yet to become fashionable, but driven by discomfort, I paid no mind to what fellow passengers might think of my behavior.

On the plane, a large man in a dark suit with a striped tie knotted at the base of a starched white collar sat down beside me, fastened his seat belt, crossed his legs, and immediately opened his newspaper. I crossed my legs and reached for my book. As the stewardess made her rounds, my seatmate ordered two Bloody Marys, which he drank in quick succession without taking his eyes from the paper. At dinner, he dabbed his lips with the cocktail napkin and finally turned his head in my direction.

"I was afraid I would end up sitting next to you," he growled.

I was instantly mortified and felt a blush creeping across my face. Even though I am an avant-garde performance artist, I cannot stand being weird and want every single person on the entire planet to think I am wonderful and be ecstatic to end up sitting next to me anywhere.

"I saw you in the airport," he went on, "and I thought darn, I'm gonna end up sitting next to that crazy lady and darned if I didn't."

I managed to whisper without looking at him that my back had been hurting. He lowered his fork and turned toward me and I turned toward him, and for the first time in the three hours that had passed with us sitting so close our shoulders rubbed, I saw human care in his eyes. "Feeling any better?" he asked, and he offered me an aspirin, which I politely declined. Realizing I wasn't completely bonkers, he started a conversation, and realizing he wasn't the movement police, I responded, and by the time we started our descent, we had become friends. As we unsnapped our seat belts, we said a warm goodbye to each other, and then he took a deep breath and asked, "By the way, where can I learn some of those stretches you were doing?" His back had been bothering him as well—an old football injury. The part of my seatmate that desired freedom had recognized the part of me that desired freedom and there we sat, no longer enemies but unlikely colleagues in our search for true comfort.

When we are true to ourselves, each of us becomes a light for another to follow.

The Bidding of the Body

If we pay close attention to sensations in the body, we detect the constant aris-ing of impulses to move—to raise an arm or drop a shoulder, to dip a knee or roll the hips. By listening and responding to these impulses, which occur mo-ment to moment as long as we are alive, we discover that we are dancing. Per-haps the dance is a walk through the woods, arms swinging boldly. Perhaps the dance is a quiet swaying as we wait in line at the movie theater. Perhaps the dance is a Zorba-the-Greek jig on a pristine beach leaving footprints on wet sand. Perhaps the dance is a wild flip-flopping, foot-stomping, hip-swinging, head-rolling, sweat-dripping nightclub romp. No matter. While dancing, the dominance of the intellect is hijacked and we find ourselves fully embodied and suddenly content. But we forget to move. Fortunately, we can find our way back to the body without undue effort, and through our recovery of the grace inherent in the body, we lay the groundwork for grace in the way we walk, and exercise, and talk, and make love, and sing, and party, and meditate.

The Practice

Close your eyes and let your attention slide into your body (like swal-lowing one of those minicameras doctors use to look at your insides) and feel what is going on. Feel the aches and the pulls and the pres-sure and the buzz of it all and then, with your eyes still closed, move. Relieve what hurts, release what is holding. Perhaps the head wants to fall forward to soften a tight area of the neck. Perhaps the arms want to lift to open the shoulders. Move for one minute, sitting at your desk, or lying in bed, or standing in your living room, or waiting on the side of the road for the AAA man to change your tire.

Respond to all calls of the body to relieve tension, contraction, or pain. Lengthen, stretch, ripple, roll, fold, bend, rock. If you're in public and don't want to move in a big way, move in a tiny way. But move.

Relieving tension in the body also relieves tension in the mind. I
think airports should have minidiscos or wandering mariachi bands offering salsa lessons so people could dance while waiting in those holding areas where everyone is nervous and fidgeting with newspapers
and guzzling martinis. The mind and the body are not separate, and
despite our efforts to think our way into well-being, we fall short of
residing in comfort if we do not listen to the bidding of our bodies.

I was hired recently to give a corporate training in creativity and stress reduc-
tion for a local dot-com start-up. The first session was for the executive team,
and I began with movement exercises—a primary and well-documented tool
for relieving stress. As I led the group through a series of gentle movements,
one of the participants scowled with unrepentant displeasure; another suddenly headed for the bathroom; another stepped into the hallway to use his
cell phone. One man made his way to the side of the room and sat down in a
chair against the wall. I approached him during a break and asked how he was
doing.

"Fine," he said. "But, frankly, I don't like to dance or do any of this stuff.
I'll watch."

He was considerably overweight and clearly uneasy with his physicality.

"You might like to learn how to move more freely," I suggested.

"Why?" he asked.

"You would be happier," I said. I like to think of myself as someone who
has the wisdom to let people decide for themselves what makes them happy,
but the words slipped out.

"I'm perfectly happy," he replied. "I've been repressed all my life and I like
it like that."

His words startled me and I wasn't convinced he believed them himself.
Nor was I convinced that I had any advice that might be of any use to him. All
I knew was that many wonderful people I have had the honor of working with
over the years have been unable to roll their shoulders or swivel their hips,

kick their legs or ripple their spines, and they have given up this freedom of movement without a whisper of protest.

For millions of years of human evolution, a sedentary lifestyle was not an option. In many parts of the world still, people walk considerable distances, throw and gather fishnets, squat on their haunches for long conversations, scale tree trunks, dig the earth, toss seed, and harvest food. In the ordinary chores of daily life, they display an ease in their movement, the skeleton loose in its sheath of muscles. Most of us have lost this ease as tension stiffens our bodies. But each of us has the capacity for physical grace, and by taking even one minute each day, we can rediscover our freedom of movement.

Trance

Many years ago, I was traveling in Guatemala and made my way to the mountain village of Todos Santos for All Saints Day. Believing that the veil, which separates the spirit world from the world of the living, is parted during these days, the villagers gather in the cemetery to commune with their ancestors. Musicians migrate with their marimbas from grave to grave throughout the days and nights and the villagers—the men in black waistcoats, flat-brimmed straw hats, and finely embroidered pants of brilliant colors; the women in long dark skirts and striped red blouses with bright cummerbunds—pray, chant, picnic, make offerings, drink the local moonshine, and dance.

I stood apart from the celebrants, observing the rituals with the kind of curious perplexity the uninformed bring to the exotic. Two toothless old women, their spines hunched, their faces carved with wrinkles, their gray hair twisted into braids, held hands as they bobbed about on a grave now littered with orange peels and eggshells and bread crumbs. Noticing me noticing them, they extended their hands and invited me to join them. I could not refuse. I held their stiff and swollen fingers and together the three of us stamped our feet to the lilting rhythm of the marimbas and danced with the ancestors.

Towering over their small, bent bodies, I thought of my own grandmother Belle, who was delayed at Ellis Island because her X rays showed dark spots. And my grandfather Herman, who smoked unfiltered cigarettes and prayed facing east each morning wrapped in his phylacteries. And my mother's father, Zvi, who devoted his life to studying and teaching the Torah. And my grandmother Ima, who bought stock, after her husband died, for pennies a share that split and tripled, but still she lived like a pauper convinced she was poor and sang "America the Beautiful" in her rocking chair. And further back, the nameless ancestors who were left behind in the old country and not remembered. They appeared now, dancing in the cemetery with me and the Indian grandmothers and their ancestors, the stream of us being born and dying and dancing.

In most cultures worldwide, dancing is a method for contacting spirit, a way of praying. Dervish dancers, one arm extended to heaven, one to earth, twirl for hours, their long robes flaring from the waist. The priestesses of Condomblé, dressed in white, dance until, overcome, they fall into trance and flail with spirit. African dancers enact planting and seduction and healing and rain as master drummers whip up a trance with their hands of fire. And thousands and thousands of young people all over the world in overalls and miniskirts and pink hair and eyebrow studs and fluorescent neckbands and bold tattoos gather at midnight in unmarked warehouses and dance until dawn to the ceaseless beat of technica. The list of people who understand how to commune with the sacred through the body of flesh and bone goes on and on.

As children, all of us knew how to go into trance: we spun and spun and spun until, no longer able to stay upright, we fell to the ground, and the world swirled around us in a kaleidoscope of wallpaper and picture frames and ceiling lamps and bureaus and siblings and family dinners and report cards and spelling bees and pigtails and binder paper, and we rested in the still center of all things. We have not forgotten how to go into trance while dancing, how to surrender our bodies to prayer; but we refrain.

To recover dance as a pathway to the sacred, all we need do is to do it— whenever, however, wherever we want, alone or together, indoors or out; all we need do is to dance.

Three Secrets

There are three secrets to enjoying yourself as you dance:

1.   Commit to what you are doing, whatever it is. If you are simply waving a hand in the air, pay attention to that movement, feel it, believe in it. Even the most basic and common gesture can be of great interest if you commit your- self fully to its execution. If we stop to analyze what is involved in move- ment, the complex biochemistry of the brain sending signals to muscle and bone, we understand that any movement is a miracle. And if we pay atten- tion, we can feel the miracle of consciousness in the moving body.

I have heard that when Mick Jagger dances, even at a small gathering of close friends, he is so deeply concentrated, so uncompromised in his ability to focus, that he appears to be engaged in serious work. A good dancer, feel- ing the body in the body, allows himself to be fascinated with his experience of dancing.

2.   Don't care if you are good at movement or bad at movement. We are raised in a culture that values expertise over exploration. As we mature, we limit ourselves to the activities we have developed considerable skill at, relegating an entire realm of human experience to others. To reclaim what we have lost, we need to understand that our success is not in the perfect execution of a triple pirouette or a flying waltz, but in having the courage to go to the

place where we are the least skilled and to explore that edge for a while. Once we feel where we are rigid and stuck, we have made the first step toward moving beyond our limits.

3.   When you feel confused on your feet, rather than trying to push away the confusion, dive headlong into the morass. When you feel awkward, rather than trying to be graceful, forge deeply into awkwardness. When you feel stuck, rather than trying to be free, melt into the center of stuckness. When you feel discomfort, rather than longing for comfort, surrender to uneasiness. Be more confused, more awkward, more stuck, more uncomfortable until you fully dissolve into the heart of these feelings. In the core of the place you have most avoided, the most unpleasant feelings dissolve and in their wake, the wildness erupts inside you and insists on speaking itself through your body.

Run and Jump

Often the most challenging part of dancing is knowing how to begin. Once we get going, movement can flow, but we are not sure how to start. We want to know what we will do before we do it, but the mind cannot come up with an idea for movement so we stand on the sidelines, waiting until we feel inspired enough, secure enough, to move out onto the floor and let our limbs take over. The liability of waiting and thinking is that movement is generally not imagined in the mind, but felt in the body, so those of us who hover on the edge, hesitating until we feel brave enough to jettison ourselves into movement, are caught in one of life's annoying paradoxes: we want to know how we are going to move before we begin moving, but in order to know how to move, we have to begin moving.

I remember as a child learning to jump rope. Two friends held the ends of the rope and together, twirled it. I stood several yards away tracing the movement of the circling rope with my hands in order to get the feel of the rhythm

in my body. At some point, I had to let go of any attempt to mentally understand my actions, and run and jump, hoping my body knew enough to behave
so that the rope would be cresting over my head as I took my place between
my friends, and that my feet would leap just as the rope slapped the ground
beneath me. I discovered that skipping rope was easy only if I let go of trying
to figure it out and allowed my body to take over. This loss of mental grasping
was both the most terrifying and the most pleasurable moment of the entire
experience of rope jumping. You can apply the same lesson to learning to ride
a bicycle and to water skiing and to making love: let the body know what it
knows. Do not get in the way.

It is the very movement from mental control into body awareness that is
the joy of physical activity, and yet, no matter how accomplished we might be
at dancing or ski jumping or swan dives, the moment of taking the leap from
mind to body, from conceptual understanding to trust, can be accompanied
by fear.

When we watch an athlete or a dancer, we have the impression that their
movements are effortless. We perceive this quality of ease because in truth,
when an athlete or dancer is working optimally, the sense of effort completely
vanishes—they have learned to work from the ground of being rather than the
effort of exertion. We, too, can learn to step aside as the ones who control unfolding reality, and allow reality to unfold through us; and when we do, fear
vanishes. And we vanish as well, we disappear into the dance and it is not we
who are dancing at all, but being, being dancing. And this is what we marvel at
when we see a great athlete or dancer or animal move—we marvel at being
dancing.

The Practice

Put on music that has a good strong beat and feel the rhythm enter your body. Then, without thinking, surrender your mind to the body and abandon yourself to movement. Whenever you start to think about what you are doing, take the attention back to the body, over and over and over again.

The next time you find yourself at a dance—a bar mitzvah or wedding or party or club—stand on the side and feel the beat. Then, without thinking, run out onto the dance floor and jump into movement. Trust your body. Do not think about it. Run and jump.

Growing an Impulse

I ran, I jumped, some of you might be saying to me just now, having put the book down and hefted yourself up from the couch, put on music and felt the beat enter your body just like you were supposed to. And then you decided to go ahead and start dancing. You threw an arm in the air or jutted a hip sideward, but you had no idea what to do next so you stood there frozen and stiff. You focused your mind on your body but nothing happened and your body felt like a big lump. Now what?

If you find yourself stuck, you are trying too hard. Dancing is easy, but only if you let dancing be easy. Try this:

The Practice

Stand still and for a moment rest fully in that stillness. Then, begin a very small, very easy (let me repeat that word: easy) movement that you can do over and over again. You might tap your foot, or rock your head from side to side, or roll a shoulder. Focus your attention on *feeling* the movement, on allowing the movement a life of its own.

Enlarge the movement by one little degree. If you are tapping a foot, you might lift the foot a bit off the floor. If you are rolling a shoulder, make a bigger rolling motion. Invest this easy (and I repeat, easy) movement with your energy and attention.

Enlarge the movement again. If you are tapping your foot and lifting it slightly off the ground, lift it higher off the ground. If you are rolling your shoulder, start to roll your entire arm.

Develop the movement incrementally, larger and larger, with more and more ease, until your whole body is involved in moving and you are traveling across the floor, and even then keep expanding the movement until you are working as fully and physically as possible with exuberance and no effort at all, not even the slightest bit because effort does not help. Remember, you already know how to dance, all you have to do is to find the path, and the path hides the moment you start to *work* at finding it.

When you reach the limit of effortless grandiosity, begin to diminish the movement, gradually, one step at a time, until you return to the small movement that launched you. Experiment with how small the movement can become and still be a movement. Perhaps an observer standing several feet away would not be able to detect that you are still moving, but internally, the movement abides.

Finally, reach a complete stillness, and in that stillness feel the resonance, the pleasure, of having moved that is alive in the quiet of the body.

A small gesture can lead to an entire range of movement experiences if you allow yourself to go along for the ride. The trick is to refrain from "inventing" movement with the mind, and to allow yourself to move without thinking. But this is not a passive exercise—you have to add fuel, and the highest octane is pure presence.

As with all forms of meditation, the point is not to space out and drift into dullness, but to become fully present. Do not hold back. Be vigorous, playful, generous. Offer your body on the altar of dance, and the dance gods will reward you with the sensual pleasure that is the birthright of all beings.

Circling

When I was twenty-two, I was invited to join Margaret Jenkins's fledgling dance company. Despite having studied dance since childhood, I was incapable of remembering complicated sequences of movement. Luckily, the postmodern movement was emerging. Now, instead of having to learn steps to precise rhythms a choreographer counted out loud as she flew through impossibly complex sequences of turns and leaps and lifts and flutters, dancers followed enthusiastic choreographic instructions like "Walk across the room pounding your feet and once in a while fall down" or "Shift your weight from one foot to another while you scratch your chin and then cross your arms."

For one piece, Margie asked me to move only in circles. Under the glare of theater lights, I spun like a top while describing circles in the air with my arms, and then I lunged in a circle around the circumference of the room. Next I made loops of tangential circles while twirling my index fingers. I felt like water flowing, like the earth rotating on its axis, like the planets revolving around the sun, like a riptide, like a toilet flushing. I realized, *Oh, this is what Tai Chi is about, this energy of circles in the universe and in the body.* And I realized that the body enjoys circles and that the joints—shoulder, hip, ankle, wrist, neck, fingers—are designed to circle. I kept coming upon new discoveries each time I performed, so I didn't stop circling when the performances were over, but kept it up in nightclubs and in my studio and surreptitiously in the grocery store while I waited on line, and in the backyard when the sun was out, and sometimes, with just my hands, in the bathtub.

To move well, we must be engaged not only physically, but also with our awareness, in the act of moving. When we watch someone move, we see not only the physical movement but we also see consciousness. We see consciousness enter the spine, or an arm, or a leg. We see when a person moves but is not "in the body." We see where a person has access to ease of movement and where the body seems restricted, unconscious.

What is remarkable is how visible awareness is. We do not need to exert any particular effort to perceive awareness in the body; we are always seeing awareness, or the lack of it, in one another's physicality, but are not usually conscious of what we are seeing. We might notice a graceful person and remark on her gracefulness, or simply know that we are attracted to someone and not understand it is because he moves with an integrated sense of physicality.

A chant I learned from an Afro-Cuban drummer goes:

> *Oye la rhumbera, oye la*
> *Oye la la rhumba, oye la.*

Which means, loosely translated:

> *Look at the dancer, see her;*
> *Look at the dance, see it.*

We see the dancer and we see the dance; they are separate but inseparable. We see the dancer enter the dance and the dance enter the dancer.

To enter the dance we must become interested in the way our bodies feel, interested in what our bodies *want* to do and what our bodies are capable of doing. The deeper we are able to feel the sensations of the dance, the more interested we become in dancing. The more interested we become in our own movement, the more interesting the movement becomes.

To meditate, one is given a focus of concentration: count the breath from one to ten, or gaze at a candle flame or pay attention only to what one is hearing. Having a task to do while meditating connects our awareness to what is actually going on moment to moment in our bodies and our minds. In the same way, having a task to do while moving tethers the mind to the body so that we are not so easily distracted and do not lose awareness of how we are moving.

Circling gives the mind a task to focus on and brings awareness into the realm of felt experience. And circling, while simple to execute, provides us with an endless experiment so that if we find ourselves on a dance floor unable to "think" of anything to do, we can circle.

The Practice

Make circles. Make circles with body parts and make circles in the room.

Allow one circling movement to flow into the next without stopping. Circling is fluid and one of the ways the movement gives us pleasure is in how it flows. Let the movement flow.

Circle to music. Circle with a friend. Circle outside. At a club or a party or in the park. Spin until you fall down. When you are sitting at your desk in front of the computer and your back is stiff, circle the spine, the shoulders, the head. When you are lying on your back on the beach, circle your arms in the sea breeze. When you are standing in the five-items-only line at the health food store with a power bar and a carrot juice in your basket and the person in front of you has a carton of eggs, six limes, a bag of black rice, a six-pack of root beer, a bag of potatoes, a hunk of cheese, peppermint dental floss, and three mangoes and you want to tap her on the shoulder and say, "Hey, can't you read?" circle your hips and roll your eyes. Relief requires only a minute of movement.

When we circle, we participate in the moving universe and we feel that we belong here, among stars and planets and oceans and rubber bands; among evaporation and spirals and flight patterns; among birth and death and sugar cookies and pulsing blood. When we circle, we find ourselves at the center of all things and at the same time, we find ourselves circumambulating the holy mountain.

Hand Dance

At a meeting with a New York publisher, I was asked which practice in this book was my favorite.

"I like all of them," I said, going totally blank and not remembering any of the practices at all. "Let's hand dance," I suggested, grabbing at something that came to mind, something we could actually *do* rather than just talk about since that is the whole point, the doing.

The editor paused, and then, with some reluctance, agreed. She rose from her seat and closed the door to her office so that none of her colleagues would see her.

"What do I do?" she asked.

"Dance with your hands," I said.

A puzzled look crossed her face and I knew that she was attempting to figure out what moves she would do before she began.

"Don't think about it. Move your hands without any mental interference," I said.

"Can I close my eyes?" she asked.

"Of course."

"Then you have to close your eyes, too," she insisted.

The editor, her publicist, my agent, and I sat with our eyes closed so as not to embarrass one another, and hand danced. But I cheated. I squinted through my nearly closed eyes and watched four grown women, all dressed in dark suits, waving their hands about on the twenty-third floor of a Manhattan high-rise.

"That felt wonderful," the editor said when we were done, and the publicist and my agent agreed, and everyone seemed surprised.

We tend to treat our hands poorly, insisting they engage in repetitive movements at keyboards, steering wheels, dinner tables for hours on end without a break. Our hands occasionally resort to primitive forms of protest, sending a shiver of pain through our joints. We respond by treating our complaining appendages to ergonomic wrist pads and chiropractic adjustments, hot pads, cold packs, muscle relaxants.

But we do not let them dance. Dancing is forbidden. We believe enterprises that are not difficult or aerobic or wealth-producing or intellectually complex or explicitly erotic are of no value, so we are startled when easy games that are mindless and quick actually evoke instant pleasure.

The Practice

Move the hands, however they feel like moving. You can do mini-hand-dances, moving only your fingers, as your wrist rests on the keyboard or the desk or the steering wheel. Or, you can include the entire hand and the lower arm. If you're feeling very shy, you can keep the hands on your lap. You can hand dance while talking on the telephone, or lying in the bathtub, or walking on the beach.

You might move only one hand at a time, and let the other respond as if your hands were having a conversation. You might move your fingers very quickly, or very slowly. Your hands might touch and get deeply entangled in one another, or never touch and remain quite distant. You might invent your own shapes with your fingers and palms. You might let your hands fly into the air, or shimmy or wave. You might find it hard to begin. Begin anyway. You might find it hard to stop. You don't have to.

Tibetan monks and nuns perform mudras while they chant, moving their hands in a symbolic language so that their prayers are integrated into the body.

Our hands are our tools for doing—we make ourselves known in the world by what we make with our hands, and what we do with our hands has a powerful effect on our subconscious. When we take time to hand dance, the message our subconscious receives is about relaxation and play and relief and prayer and vacation. Even a moment of hand dancing has a profound effect. For that moment, we have been in Tahiti, hula dancing on a beach; for that moment, we have entered a holy place and offered prayer; for that moment, we have given our hearts and our minds respite.

Tree Dance

My movement training began when I was four and my mother enrolled me in a modern dance class for toddlers held in the garage studio of a fifties ranch-style house on a suburban cul-de-sac. I wore a skirt that billowed as I crossed the floor in a pack of preschoolers, falling, rolling, crawling.

"This is how we are bugs," the teacher said in a spasm of delight, creeping along the floor with her fingers splayed and her elbows bent and protruding.

We were forced to imitate her.

"This is how we are elephants," she uttered with terrifying enthusiasm as she curved over, her arms interlaced and swinging between her legs like a trunk.

Since then, I have shivered in horror when anyone suggested I dance like a sunset or a hurricane or a dolphin. But then I came upon tree dancing and for some unknown reason, I've taken to the practice.

The initial inspiration arose one summer while I was living on land in the foothills of the northern Sierras owned by Mel Hendersen. Mel is a sculptor. He is also a gold miner, as was his father, and spends his summers underground with a couple of mining partners digging for a vein they know runs somewhere through the vast property.

Mel built a bed for me under a stand of four tall pines, and I set up an outdoor kitchen. Each afternoon, I lugged large plastic bottles down the steep trail to Indian Creek, which ran cold through the valley of meadows, and collected my supply of water. During my daily hikes, I came across tree stumps, the remains of timber Mel had felled to build the ramparts of the mine. One day, I stepped onto a stump and, with my feet planted firmly as if rooted, I began to dance. I didn't pretend to be a tree, but I felt treelike, as if wind were moving through branches, moving me. The sensation of rocking my torso and limbs, first gently and then more vigorously while my feet remained still, was surprisingly compelling, surprisingly comforting. So during my weeks of living on the land, I often jumped atop stumps to dance.

If we look deeply, we begin to recognize that all our mental and physical activity arises from a still place. Out of silence, sound arises. Out of stillness, movement arises. The tree dance is a physical metaphor for the inextricability of stillness from movement and movement from stillness.

At the end of my summer in the foothills, I was scheduled to give a performance at the university art gallery in Davis. Mel loaded my station wagon with tree stumps of varying heights, and I spent the afternoon arranging them on the polished wooden floor of the gallery. I began my performance dancing on a tree stump and contemplating the interconnected web of tree, limbs, stump, wood floor, bodies, dancing, death, and transformation.

We do not exactly die, Thich Nhat Hanh said during one of his dharma talks. Our bodies return to their original elements, becoming water and earth; the water evaporates and turns into rain that falls on the earth; the earth is transformed into carrots and cabbages and beets and apple trees that contain parts of us; the people and animals who eat the cabbage and the carrots and the beets and the apples are eating elements that contain part of us, and our elements become a part of them. We do not exactly die, but we continue on and on in this life—as air and wind and water and carrots and apples and tree stumps and people dancing on top of tree stumps, and so come to know who we are.

Recently, during a meditation retreat, I climbed a hillside of dry and shining grasses and stood looking out at the rolling hills below me. The sky was a bold winter blue. A wind blew across from the coast and cooled my bare arms. Sunshine doused me. I planted my feet on the ground and I tree danced, moving my limbs above the base of my steady feet. I felt how the sky and the grasses and the old oak a few yards away all carried rhythms that my body could feel, and I danced to that cadence. We are accustomed to dancing with a partner and to music, but we can also dance to the rhythm and the touch of sun and wind and rain and starlight and allow them entrance to the body.

Sometimes I tree dance indoors. The body sways, undulates, ripples above a base of stillness; feelings arise and pass away, moving the body; and the body rooted in the earth, dances.

The Practice

Stand with your feet hip-width apart, close your eyes, and plant your feet into the ground. Allow movement to arise, as if a wind is blowing and moving you. Perhaps a wind is in fact blowing. Allow the breath of wind to move your body. Arms might lift. Fingers might ripple. The torso might sway from side to side.

Allow more vigorous movement to arise. Keep the feet planted. As you move, feel the earth below you and the sky above you and allow the earth and the sky to enter your movement. Let the weather enter your movement, and the light. Let the grasses and birds and rocks enter your movement. Let the trees enter your movement.

When you are ready, find your way to stillness.

A Moment of Movement

Upon occasion, I remember to dance. Upon occasion, I remember to get up from the computer, or hang up the phone, or pause before washing the dishes, and I play music and dance around my room, alone and unobserved. Upon occasion, I remember that no matter what state of mind I am in when I begin, I always feel better when I dance. Sometimes I cannot bring myself to dance, cannot break the hypnotic trance that binds me to sitting, driving, Web surfing, e-mailing, conversing. Sometimes the memory of dancing that nestles in bone and tendon and muscle and synapse insists that no matter what else I imagine needs to occupy my time, I must, for a minute, dance.

The Practice

Get up and dance. Be awkward. Be graceful. Be quirky. Be yourself. Find movements you have never done before, movements that are idiosyncratic, uncomfortable, off-kilter. Find movements you love to do, have done for years. Do large movements with the whole body, grand sweeps of the arms and legs. Do small movements with only a small part of the body, like a finger or an elbow. Travel across the room and back. Or occupy only a tiny space.

Extend the arms and reach to the very ends of the fingertips and feel the spine lengthen as you reach, and reach out of the top of your head. We rarely stretch to the extent of our capacity. Stretching to the limits of our ability feels regal and proud and powerful and satisfying.

Dance to all kinds of music, not just music you believe is danceable. All music is danceable. You will move in an entirely different way to Chopin than to the Rolling Stones or Miles Davis or the women of

Mali. You will find characters alive inside of you whom you have never met before because you have never found a way for them to come out of hiding.

Be elegant. Be stupid. Be silly. Be ridiculous. Be ungainly. Be erotic. Or not. Invent. Or copy, doing what you saw someone else do and wanted to try when no one was looking. Close your eyes. Open your eyes. Dance with your reflection in the sliding glass door. Dance with your shadow. Dance with your dog or the rosebush. For one minute, or two, or five your job is to dance.

three

To Sing Like a River

Opening the Voice

"There was a time when the loudest sound was the sound of the village chanting. We've gone from a world full of sound—bird song, wind in the trees, insects, people chanting—to a world filled by the noise of machines where we are silent. All science tells us that we are resonant. If it is a resonant world and we are resonant beings, singing and chanting are ways to communicate, to exchange ourselves with the world. And the voice is the one thing we no longer use."

—JILL PURCE

Sounding the Body

Last year at a conference where I had been invited to give a performance, Bri Maya Tiwari told the story of her remarkable recovery from ovarian cancer. A stunning woman who had worked in the fashion industry in New York, she was diagnosed with the disease when in her early twenties. After several surgeries and rounds of radiation treatment, the doctors had told her that the cancer was still rampant and that she could expect to live for only two months. Bri Maya retreated alone to the woods to die "with dignity." She told us how she moved into a tiny cabin and spent her days meditating, eating according to Aryuvedic principles, resting, attuning to the natural cycles of her environment, and chanting. She attributes her extraordinary remission in part to her chanting. Upon finishing her talk, she stood, radiant in the middle of the huge stage decades after her terminal diagnosis, and let out a healthy "Ooouuummmm."

Bri Maya founded a center in North Carolina where every morning she goes outside and chants in the fields. The cows, she says, chant with her. At first, they mooed on several different pitches, but after some months, their voices tuned to hers, and now Bri Maya reports that the cows have joined her in chanting "Ooouuummm."

While I do not suggest that anyone forego treatments provided by allopathic medicine, I do recommend that we acknowledge and act upon what we know in our hearts and from our own experience to be true: that vocalizing is good for our physical, mental, and spiritual health.

Sound is created by waves that create vibrations, and hearing happens when these vibrations resonate against our eardrums. But our eardrums are not the only parts of our bodies that are affected. Our bones resonate with sound vibrations, as do our organs, our brains and even our skin, and so we can barely sit still when music with a lively beat is playing; we have to at least shuffle our feet or wag a finger because the music, literally, is shaking us. We are vibrated by sounds that we hear and by sounds that we make with our own voices. Jerzy Grotowski, the renowned Polish director of experimental theater, had his actors practice vocalizing for hours each day, refining their ability to resonate distinct body parts: knees, elbows, belly, back, index finger, left toe. By learning to pulsate body parts with sound, his actors developed remarkable versatility with their voices that allowed for an enormous range of self-expression.

Schools of medicine have arisen that utilize the making of sound as a healing practice, particularly in the East. According to Aryuvedic medicine, the voice, by resonating organs and bones, can be used to free blockages in the flow of energy through our bodies, thereby establishing a physical environment where the body's own powers of repair can operate unimpeded.

The Practice

Lie on your back or sit comfortably in a chair or on a pillow. Lay the palms of your hands on your lower abdomen, below your waist, and allow your breath to deepen so that the belly rises and falls with the coming and going of breath. When you feel the breath is centered in the belly, begin producing a very gentle "ahhhhhh" tone with the voice. Feel the belly vibrate with the sound you are making. Experiment with lowering the tone of your voice since a deeper tone resonates more easily in the belly than a high tone. Imagine the intestines, the reproductive organs vibrating with sound.

Place the hands so that they rest over the ribs, and feel breath expand the rib cage. Make an "ahhhhhh" tone, and imagine the bones, the liver, the kidneys, the spleen, the gall bladder, and the stomach vibrating with sound.

Place the palms of the hands on the chest. Feel the breath fill the lungs, which extend to the tips of the shoulders. Begin to sound, feeling the chest vibrate under your hands. Imagine the lungs and the heart vibrating.

Place the palms over the eyes. Feel the breath enter through the nostrils, and imagine the breath filling the head. Send sound into the cavities of the skull: the sinus passages and eye sockets and mouth. Imagine the sound vibrating the brain and the seams of the skull. You might want to experiment with an "eeeee" vowel (as in "me") and work with a higher pitch.

When you are finished, rest for a moment and feel the effects of the sounding. Often there is a feeling of relaxation and spaciousness in the body that is quite remarkable.

You can do this exercise in a few minutes, resting in each body part for thirty seconds as you move up the torso. Or you can devote ten minutes to the practice. If you are suffering from an illness or chronic pain, you might want to devote more time, moving slowly and carefully through the body and focusing on particular parts that draw your attention.

Listening

I first learned about listening as a meditation practice during a workshop with the composer Pauline Oliveros. On the first morning of the workshop, Pauline instructed us to close our eyes and listen—just listen. Initially, I became aware of the most prominent sounds: the roar of a passing car, the cough of a fellow student. Then I began to hear sounds that I ordinarily would not notice: the buzz of the fluorescent lights, the ticking of a clock. As the minutes passed and my listening became even more refined, I heard the sounds of my own body: breathing, swallowing, rumbling. The hum of the air conditioner

and the drone of a passenger jet produced separate pitches that together created harmonies; rhythms emerged. I realized that I was locating sound in
space as I was hearing it in time, and that sound was occurring within my consciousness and in the exterior environment in a continuum that had no de-
tectable boundaries.

What Pauline was teaching us, not by explanation but by directing us to
our own experience, was the presence of sound, how we are drenched in
sound whether or not we are aware of it. By listening with attention, we notice the range and variety, texture and musicality, complexity and interrela-
tionship of the sounds that are an essential and constant element of our lives;
and as we turn to the making of sound with our voices and instruments, our
vocabulary and our understanding of composition is enormously expanded.
To compose well, Pauline taught us, we must be able to listen well. But listening well is not for composers alone—listening is for anyone interested in
a fully sensual life.

Years later when I was in India, I had another memorable sound experience. I
was on my way to see H. W. L. Poonja, an enlightened master who was re-
puted to have great powers of transmission. I didn't believe in gurus, but
many of my friends had returned from visits with this teacher aglow with
well-being and I couldn't help but be intrigued, so I decided to extend a
trekking trip to Nepal and visit his home in Lucknow.

With the assistance of Indian friends in Delhi who were intimate with the
intricacies of the rail system, I had made train reservations well in advance.
My friends dropped me off at the Delhi station close to midnight and instructed me to look for a paper posted on a pole where I would find my name
and car assignment. Sure enough, my name was typed neatly into a numbered
rectangle. I was booked on a second-class, air-conditioned sleeper, upper
bunk, the car of choice according to my fat and, by now, dog-eared guidebook. As the train screeched into the teeming station, I hurried through the
bustling crowd of Sikhs in white turbans, and Hindus with caste marks on

their foreheads, and Muslims in veils, and businessmen in suits, and homeless boys in rags, and sadhus in nearly nothing.

Maneuvering through the press of humanity, I made my way up and down, up and down the track unable to locate my car. A Sikh, who had been assigned to the same mysteriously absent coach, grabbed my elbow. "It is missing," he said with a high voice and a wobble of his turbaned head, and since not a single second-class sleeper had been coupled onto the chain, he hastened me through the jam of characters rushing for car doors and guided me into a third-class sleeper where I scrambled onto an upper bunk. Four more men piled into the tiny compartment behind us and within minutes, the floor was scattered with peanut shells and medallions of spilled chai and red betel spit. I had been assured by my Indian friends that bedding would be provided, but the bunk was torn and bare so I pulled out a thin shawl and, embracing my suitcase to protect it from middle-of-the-night theft (since I had forgotten to purchase a lock and chain as prescribed by the guidebook), I pretzeled myself into the narrow bed.

As the train squealed out of the depot, an icy wind whistled through the windows, which refused to close, that cut straight to the bone. The men around me snored and coughed, spit and wheezed. Shivering, I curled up more tightly under my shawl and tried fruitlessly to sleep as the onset of sickness approached with its flare of warning signals: a stab of pain accompanied each swallow, my nose dribbled, my chest ached. As the hours wore on, I shifted restlessly from one cramped position to another, fantasizing all manner of horrors: how I would end up in a noisy Indian hospital room lying alone with a salami-size IV needle delivering massive doses of antibiotics along with exotic diseases into my wracked body while hordes of everyone else's family members camped out on the floor; how my suitcase would be stolen even though I was intertwined with it in a Tantric embrace; how I would forget the warnings in the guidebook never to eat candy handed to you by strangers because, more likely than not, they are laced with drugs that stupefy you for days, long enough for anyone to do anything at all to you and your stuff. At this point I recycled back to the hospital room where doctors discovered I was missing precious organs that had been auctioned off to international traders.

Near dawn, however, I found myself adrift in a field of music. The rumble of wheels modulated to a sweet humming and grew to lyrical heights. Medleys greeted our arrival at each depot—the dipthonged chants of food vendors, the high drone of braking wheels, the elongated call of train whistle like a muezzin's prayer—melodies blending in a sweep of perfect harmonics, moving in sublime variations, reducing my physical suffering to a background blur. Finally, accompanied by a lullaby of chai wallahs, I fell asleep.

I could not help but notice an extraordinary shift in my perception of reality. My surroundings, once glaring with the threat of physical danger and human malice, had become sublime. Whether or not this transfiguration was due to an exotic psychic power the guru was exerting over my consciousness or if I had merely become so exhausted that my mind, in its near-sleep daze, had modulated to receive sound in an unimpeded way, I will never know. What I do know is that when we become quiet enough, the universe displays its panoply of wonders that until then have been masterfully camouflaged as the most mundane of events.

The Practice

Close your eyes and focus on hearing. Listen to the sounds that are the most obvious, then tune in to the quieter sounds. Notice the way sounds arise and pass away, moment to moment. Notice near sounds and distant ones. Avoid naming the source of the sound—wind, dog bark, fax machine—and hear the sound with clear attention. If the mind wanders, bring it back to listening again.

Listen for ten minutes, or five, or one. No matter. A convenient aspect of listening is that we can do it anywhere, any time, any place, and for as long or short a duration as we please. As long as we have ears that can hear, we have the privilege of devoting ourselves to a moment of listening.

The other day, I accompanied a friend to the hospital for her presurgical pro-
tocols. During a break, I stepped into the bathroom located off the main
lobby. As I closed the door to the stall, a deep and echoing bang reverberated
in the tiled room. When I left the stall, I closed the door, which was now the
best musical instrument at hand, a bit more vigorously. Despite the fact that I
was deeply saddened by my friend's condition, I nevertheless experienced a
moment of delight in the echoing melody of the stall door, and I wondered if
the other women in the restroom would notice the music of doors and as they
made their exit, do so with a harmonic boom.

The Cultivation of Happiness

I take a shower in the morning, every morning. The falling water, warm and
welcome, pounds against my skin. If I were to sing, naked and alone, my voice
would resonate as though a sound engineer had adjusted the tone to the most
satisfying texture of vibrations, but instead I think about cooking oatmeal and
researching a cell phone deal and how I have to swing by the ATM. If I were to
sing, the song would echo off the tile walls and the tight pull of my forehead
toward the center of my eyebrows would soften, but instead I promise myself
to make it to the gym in the afternoon but then I remember I didn't walk the
dog yesterday so replace the gym plan with the dog plan. If I were to sing, I
would be suddenly at ease, but instead I hurry a towel over my wet skin, wondering whether or not my favorite pair of blue jeans is clean or lying rumpled
in the laundry basket, and then the phone rings and I race, half-naked, to answer.

Because we are human, the urge to sing wells up in us again and again, but we
have stifled the impulse so repeatedly, alone and collectively—reaching for
the remote, opening the paper, turning on the radio in the car—that we are

now conditioned to overlook it altogether. Like a muscle group that is under-used and so atrophies, our unexercised voices have lost their strength, flexi-bility, and range. Convinced we cannot sing well, we do not sing at all; and not singing at all, we do not develop the ability to sing.

All we need do to recover our capacity for song and resonant speech is to use the full range of our voices. Even those born with the gift of a lucid voice and perfect pitch practice vocalizing to cultivate timbre, tuning, and clarity. Vocalizing is fun and the benefits immediately apparent—after only a few minutes, our voices open, and when we return to speaking, we notice a soft-ening of tone which gives us confidence in the quality of our sound produc-tion so we feel more comfortable in conversation and song. But for some, even simple vocal explorations can evoke terror.

This week, I had my students take a single phrase of text and riff with every consonant and vowel of each word. This exercise gives the performer an opportunity to explore the vocal and emotional possibilities of a text and is generally both fascinating to observe and to do as primal sounds and gestures emerge, and words take on unexpected layers of felt experience. One of the more talented students, however, sat by my side in a state of increasing anxi-ety as she witnessed the wheezing and humming and ooohhhming and shoosh-ing and ta-ta-ta-ing and the-the-the-ing of her fellow students. When Janet's turn came around, she refused to leave her seat.

"I'm not doing it," she said.

"Go ahead," I encouraged. "Experiment, play, see what comes out of your mouth. There's no right or wrong."

"I can't do it," she insisted. "Don't make me do it, just this once."

But I did make her do it, just that once, and reluctantly, Janet walked out onto the floor.

Her work was wonderful—her voice strong, her expression authentic—but the second she finished, she raced back to her seat. "I hate that exercise," she confessed as she sat down hard. "I absolutely detest it!" Sweat glistened on her neon-red face and she slumped back in her chair and closed her eyes.

"Go back out," I suggested. "Improvise about whatever comes up."

Again, she refused; again, I gently insisted; again she made her way reluctantly to the floor. Immediately, an image came rushing into her mind.

"I'm in the fourth grade," she said, "in an auditorium full of all the kids in the whole school, and I'm on stage in a chorus and singing 'God Bless America.' The teacher is sitting at the piano and has white hair and she's wearing a blue suit buttoned all the way up to the collar. She suddenly stops playing and she lurches to her feet and she screams, 'Someone is singing out of tune!' She picks four of us out of the chorus and makes us each sing alone. The first boy is wearing thick glasses and he stares at his feet and he whispers out the words and Mrs. Stratford says, 'Not you.' Then a girl sings—Nancy, that's her name, I remember her pigtails—and she squeaks out a line and Mrs. Stratford says, 'Not you.' Then it's my turn and I feel like I'm going to pee in my pants and my knees are shaking, and I manage to sing, 'God bless America, land that I love,' and Mrs. Stratford lurches toward me, pointing her finger and screaming, 'It's you!!! It's you!!!' She makes me walk all the way across the room to the orchestra and a boy hands me a triangle. I'm in a daze as I stand there, bonking the triangle—one, two, three, one, two, three—and the boy leans over and tells me I'm doing it wrong. I can't even play the damn triangle. So I just stand there, staring out into the sea of audience members and they are all staring back, right at me."

Since that time, forty years ago, Janet has refused to sing, ever, even "Happy Birthday" to her best friend.

No matter how long we have remained mute due to public humiliation or private fear, all of us can recover the capacity to produce an entire range of sounds and melodies that express our feelings and the host of characters who have taken up residence inside our psyches. When we regain the ability to feel comfortable with our voices and use them in a way that is fully expressive, we also regain vitality and amusement. Our moods are improved in part because of the psychological release gained through vocal expression, and in part because of the physiological effects of vocal resonance in the body.

Singing and sound making generate feelings of joy and optimism. Cultivating the art of happiness is one of the most profound tasks we can attend to in this life. Despite our incomparably deep attachment to being alive, we forget to relish the fact of our mere existence; we forget to celebrate this brief fling at life that each of us is given only once. Singing is a strategy for the cultivation of happiness and is available to each of us at every moment throughout our lives.

Scat Singing

To think like a mountain
And sing like a river

—MARY DE LA VALETTE

I was at a party recently, and a well-known jazz singer sat down next to me as I was munching hors d'oeuvres and introduced himself, even though I imagine he was well aware that I was well aware of who he was. Fame makes my mouth dry so the conversation did not flow easily, but the uneven dialogue didn't seem to faze him. As soon as there was a pause, he burst into a phrase of scat singing.

"I live in a large house on the lake and I love the white winters," he said, and then sang, "Di dum, da da, wha-wha-wha."

"I hate the cold," I said, feeling much too bashful to launch into a phrase of song myself—after all, he was a real singer.

"The snow sparkles, shoo ba, shoo ba, de dum," he sang.

Later when I was alone in the car, I let out a good ba ba bum, di di waah, and entertained myself all the way across the Golden Gate Bridge.

Most of our conversations would benefit by adding a bit of scatting. We might not be forthright enough to emit a round of syllabling with a stranger at a cocktail party, even though we are fully aware that such a burst would be remarkably satisfying and could transform the nature of cocktail parties and human relating worldwide—but perhaps we have the gusto to scat sing when we are alone. An inner voice will tell us that we are being ridiculous, that this is a game for children and the deranged, but I am not suggesting we reclaim our "inner child" or "inner lunatic." Frankly, I don't care about inner children or inner lunatics. I am interested in adults who, having reached a desirable level of maturity in their lives choose to sing rather than to steep in a self-induced stupor of censorship.

There are technical as well as psychological benefits to scat singing. By using our tongues and lips to shape a variety of sounds, we loosen the habitual tightness that we hold in the muscles of our face, but aren't aware of, and this relaxation affects the quality of our speech. When the muscles that produce vocal sound are relaxed, the voice resounds with a felt ease and our voices become more believable, more pliable, more open.

When we listen to a vocalist whose singing pleases us, most likely, we will notice the obvious skills—that the singer has the capacity to hit and sustain notes on pitch and keep the beat. But if we pay more careful attention, we might hear an attribute that is more difficult to name—a quality of openness, or lack of tension, that lends the voice a technical resonance as well as a feeling of emotional transparency. In the same way that we perceive holding in the body and react to it in one another, we also perceive holding in the voice and we respond by a subtle pulling away. Usually we are not conscious of this internal reaction, but we are in fact continually responding to the sound of one another's voices.

Riffs of nonverbal sounds delight us in a way that lyrics, however skillfully rendered, cannot. And while most of us are terrified at the prospect of improvising, once we allow ourselves to enter the territory of sounds and express layers of felt experience that words are unable to disclose, we enjoy the surprise of what emerges from our mouths, uncensored. Children and jazz singers understand the simple pleasure of rhythmic babbling. Ba da boom, wa waaaah. What satisfaction! And most adults, if we tell the truth, will remember the delight of lips moving and sound emerging willy-nilly that we experi-

enced as children. Doodling with the voice is what we love about Frank Sinatra, shoo be do, what we will return to if we live to be so old we forget the
rules, ba ba blu, and what we can reclaim at any age if we want to enjoy our
lives more fully, da da dum.

The Practice

When we begin to improvise with sounds, we might find that the range
of our vocabulary is dismal in its scope. We want to scat freely, but
find ourselves stuck on da-da-da, or na-na-na. The following exercise
is used by jazz vocalists to train the voice to have access to as many
sounds as possible.

Begin with the vowel "a" as in "day." Add consonants to the vowel:
way, gay, bay, nay, ray, fray, jay, blay. Go fast, go slow. Play.

Now move on to the vowel "e" as in "deed." Add consonants: we,
be, he, gee, plee, see, nee, lee. Find consonants that aren't normally
found together: hree, schnee, bldee.

Continue until you have worked with all of the long vowels: "i" as
in "bite," "o" as in "go," "u" as in "glue." You can also work with soft
vowels: "ah" as in "father," "eh" as in "bed," "uh" as in "under," "ih" as in
"winter."

Now scat—string together one-syllable sounds to make phrases.
Shoo ba de wo ba ba zoom. Work with variety, melody, and rhythm. If
you find a pattern you enjoy, repeat it for a few bars before moving on
to the next pattern. Play without effort or mental interference. Melody
and rhythmic flow and syllabic bits can unfold organically, shoo doo be
dooo.

Allow how you are feeling to penetrate the sounds: sad, happy,
tired, depressed, anxious, excited, nervous.

When you're inching along in a bottleneck of traffic, instead of listening to the radio, spew a long and beleaguered whine of syllables. While hiking, use the rhythm of walking to support a vocal improvisation. Scat sing while vacuuming, or alone in a hotel room getting ready for a business meeting. Scat your child to sleep.

Scat sing at work, while engaged in a distressing conflict, or simply so bored you can't face continuing the project at hand. Instead of checking your e-mail or shopping on-line, take a moment and scat. In the same way a Zen archer is able to hit the target by diverting his gaze as he releases the arrow, we are often able to solve problems when we divert our minds. Solutions to both technical and emotional knots arise when we soften our minds and our hearts, when we relax. And scat singing, because it is nonsense, relaxes us.

The most difficult part of scat singing is not the singing, but allowing oneself to begin. Try an experiment: each time the thought to scat crosses your mind, go ahead and sing. You need not scat for long, a moment will do. In the same way that we have conditioned ourselves *not* to sing, we can recondition ourselves *to* sing. Mental training occurs one experience at a time, and builds over weeks and months and years. Each moment that we sing encourages the next moment of song. Each moment that we sing is a moment we have spent our lives in song.

A Moment of Melody

One afternoon while I was in Lucknow, I rented a bicycle and headed for the forest on the edge of town. Three-wheeled motor taxis roared past me disgorging clouds of black exhaust into the already opaque air. Herds of water buffalo, bells clanging, lumbered down the middle of the road. Old bulbous

Russian automobiles, ignoring all lane restrictions, released a cacophony of blasting horns. And rickshaw drivers, ringing their handlebar bells, induced near-death experiences as they wove through the menagerie of traffic. The din was impressive.

I pedaled away from the big roads onto small streets lined with shacks and shaded by big-leafed trees, relieved to be free of the assault. The quiet was not the only becalming element. Passing by the bungalows of the poorest people in town, I was accompanied by singing. I could only catch a phrase or two before riding out of earshot, but then another melody down the road would catch my attention.

In India, people sang. The women sang while they washed clothes at the river, or swept the floors, or made chapatis. The rickshaw drivers sang at night, gathered around dung fires in the vacant lots where they built tent communities. Men sang while they walked to work in the mornings. Congregants sang in temples where they gathered for daily prayers and ritual pujas. Sadhus, wearing only a white cloth gathered around their loins, their beards tickling their navels, chanted as they wandered from village to village.

Inspired by the songs that were wafting through the air as I bicycled to the forest, I wanted to sing as well. I've studied singing and music theory; I've performed in an a cappella group; I've written and recorded songs. Still, fear stopped me. I didn't want to draw attention to myself, a Western woman alone on a bicycle. That was one excuse. I didn't feel like singing any of the songs I knew. That was another excuse. I wasn't inspired to make up a melody. That was the third excuse. I was bicycling through what had been reported to be a dangerous part of town; if I sang, someone might attack me. That was the fourth excuse. I could have gone on and on with reasons not to sing—good reasons, important reasons, reasonable reasons, convincing reasons, profound reasons. But finally, alone on my clunky rented bicycle and wearing a big white hat, I laughed out loud at the litany of justifications my mind was inventing to keep me from being a human who sang, just as all human beings throughout the history of our species have sung, and I sang.

The difficulty with reclaiming our voices is not that singing is difficult but

that allowing ourselves to sing requires a mustering of will, which is simultaneously a pure surrender to doing what we actually feel like doing.

The Practice

Sing. Sing a song you know from childhood that your mother sang to
you; or a song you learned when you were a teenager and listened to
so many times you still know all the words by heart, or at least the
chorus. Sing every day for a week, no matter what is happening or
where you are or how you feel or what you are thinking about. Sing
whatever song comes to mind.

At some point during the week of singing, sing really loud, so loud
that the neighbors hear you. Belt out a song with complete abandon.

At another time during the week, sing with as much feeling as you
can muster. Invite emotions to well up inside of you and come out in
the singing.

At another point during the week, sing very softly, sweetly, and let
your voice feel like it is floating on a cloud or falling through the air
like a feather that has come loose from the wing of a high-flying bird.

At some point, play around with rhythm as you sing, tapping your
foot or slapping your thigh or drumming with the fork and knife on
the table like you did when you were a teenager.

Singing has a profound effect on the way that we feel and it costs nothing. If
you are angry, burst into song. If you are feeling lively, burst into song. If you
are feeling jealous, burst into song. If you are feeling ecstatic, burst into song.
If you are feeling blue, burst into song.

I recently saw a film about cantors from around the world. A Russian cantor said that the chanting style of Eastern European Jews is often more melancholy than the musical styles of the Western Europeans. "But even sad singing
is happy," he added with a grin.

Expressing any emotion through song is a great release, and halfway through a sad song you might find yourself quite content. Or you might not know how you're feeling at all until you start singing and the song reveals yourself to yourself.

Remember: resistance is part of the game and never completely disappears. "All spiritual practice brings us face-to-face with our particular resistance. It's important to remember that resistance isn't what keeps us from our spiritual work. It is our spiritual work," writes Rabbi Avram Davis.

No matter who told us what when we were children—that we sang off-key or had bad voices, or should whisper the words—now it is our choice, as adults, to sing our way through our lives, or not.

Remember the Words, Forget the Words

When I studied voice, all my teachers made me learn songs and sing them over and over again until, fluent with the lyrics and melody, I could *feel* the song and let the feelings out through a softening here, a crescendo there, and somewhere else, a lightness. Singing is fun because song brings feelings to the surface of experience rather than relegating them to some back room because they are interfering with our functioning. We *have* to feel to sing well, and we have to let the feelings tumble and spin and croon and fly around inside the voice.

But many of us do not remember the words to songs and so do not sing at all. We can scat sing and rely on a nonverbal vocabulary for self-expression, but for those moments when we long to sing words, poetry, we need to actually learn the lyrics. So go ahead—buy a songbook, or study liner notes, or push the repeat button on your sound system and sing along to a favorite track until your housemates threaten to evict you. Practice in the car, while you're jogging, when you're on your knees in the garden pulling weeds.

Generally we are drawn to a song that expresses a feeling we are having in the moment, or have felt in the past, so that the song resonates, informing us about our own experience. Perhaps we are heartbroken and find ourselves singing, "I'm crazy, crazy for feeling so lonely." By singing the song, our feelings are expressed, ex-pressed, routed out of the chambers of the bulging, bloody heart and sent on their way into the vast and pulsating universe. We feel better.

Perhaps we are feeling quite fine. In fact, we have just fallen in love with the world's most flawless human being and cannot contain our joy, even though we know we are in a state of pure delusion. And because we have followed the suggestions in this book, we happen to have a song handy about falling madly into blind love and we sing it from the rooftops, or at least while we're sitting on the toilet.

Perhaps we are with a child who is ill or irritated or in pain. We can sing a song that soothes him or makes him laugh. Perhaps we are working with friends or colleagues, stuffing envelopes, or painting the walls, or moving to a new habitat and have to carry all of our stuff: boxes of vitamins, crates of journals we have not cracked a peek at for decades. We can sing to make us stop thinking about the fact that really, we should have had a huge garage sale followed by a bonfire.

The species depends on song for well-being. Taking the time to learn a song means that if the moment arises when a song is called for, we have one in our pocket.

> Catch a falling star and put it in your pocket
> Save it for a rainy day

However, even if you are too lazy to ever learn the lyrics to a song, you can still sing. You can make up the lyrics. And you don't need to be a great genius with the English language to make up words to sing, you need only to let the most meaningless, silly clichés fall out of your mouth unimpeded. You need only to babble senselessly and have fun. A good place to begin when you attempt to make up lyrics is right where you are:

> *I'm sittin' at my desk*
> *the one my grandma kept*
> *in her kitchen, in her kitchen,*
> *I'm lookin' out the window*
> *and the trees are dropping leaves,*
> *dropping leaves.*
> *The carpenters are pounding*
> *on the roof across the street*
> *and my dog is barking*
> *and my cat is sleeping*
> *and the mailman is walking*
> *to the rhythm of the hammers*
> *and the rhythm of the saws*
> *and the rhythm of the leaves*
> *crunching,*
> *under his feet.*

I wrote that lyric by singing it, instantly, and while it may not be a song I want to record, or sing to anyone, or even expose in print, I did have fun singing it—and I feel happier than I did just moments ago before I sang it. I've cheered myself up in a second, without Prozac or a double latte or a new lipstick.

Start where you are. In the car or on the beach, in your office or your living room or your bedroom. Notice the objects around you. You don't need to be profound or theoretical to sing. Notice the time of day or night. Notice the thoughts in your mind. Sing.

Let one phrase lead to the next. Do not judge your work, do not slow down, keep going. Repeat phrases. Repeat images. Let the rhythm support you. Sing in tune or out of tune. Notice what's going on in your life just now, at the moment, and sing that out loud.

I will repeat the guidelines: be senseless, silly, uncensored, do not judge, and sing all the while.

The Language of Love

My mother died of multiple myeloma when I was twenty-three. Until days before her death, she lived alone at home, insisting on managing without a daily caretaker. For the first two years of her illness, I visited on occasional weekends to help with the shopping and cooking and other household chores. As her condition declined, I stayed with her every weekend, assisting her in and out of bed when she needed to go to the bathroom, and afterward, when she was in her room and couldn't see me, mopping up the trail of wet tracks she had left on the floor.

One Saturday morning when I arrived, she was nearly incoherent with pain. In those days, the word "cancer" was not spoken aloud and hospice care did not exist. I tried to feed my mother fluids, one spoonful at a time. Wracked with pain, she refused to swallow and within hours slipped into delirium. Convinced the doctors knew more than I did about helping someone die, I called the ambulance and efficient strangers in uniforms slid her onto a stretcher and took her to the hospital where, eventually, she was hooked up to a morphine drip.

I did not know then how to pray or meditate at the bedside of someone who is transitioning from this life to the great beyond. I slipped in and out of the room, clueless as to how to take care of myself or my mother. My grandmother sat in a chair in the corner of the room chanting prayers under her breath, day and night, until my mother took her final breath. Then my grandmother wept and I took her home and she fixed me noodle kugel and prayed some more, tears streaking her furrowed face.

Last year, my friend Elaine, who had been battling breast cancer for twenty years, was hospitalized while I was visiting her in Mississippi. A treacherous bout of chemotherapy had left her body wasted, and she was delirious from malnutrition and medications. I sat in the hospital room for hours as she thrashed about and talked to invisible visitors. But this time, whenever I felt the impulse, I sang. I sang "Swing Low, Sweet Chariot" because I was in the South and that's what came to mind. I sang "Michael Row the Boat Ashore" because I'd seen the big river in the morning. I sang Hebrew prayers I had learned from my grandmother. By now I had learned that even when someone is so ill she cannot understand language, she can still be affected by song. Song speaks not to the intellect, but directly to the heart. And my friend loved to sing, so I suspected if she were to pull out of her near-death encounter, she would emerge with a song on her lips. Days after being released from the hospital, Elaine was sitting up in her bed at home and singing love songs.

When I was a child, my father would come into my room before I fell asleep, sit on the edge of my bed and sing, "Daisy, Daisy, tell me your answer true; I'm half crazy all for the love of you." I believed that he loved me from the center of his heart because I could hear that depth of affection in the way that he sang. Later, when he married a new wife and had a batch of new children and I saw him only on Sundays, I still remembered how he had perched on the edge of my bed at night and sung to me; how he had loved me, and must still, because the kind of love I had heard in his voice never disappears.

Having the courage to sing is not different from having the courage to love— to love ourselves and each other. I sing to my dog and my cat. I sing to my children friends. I sing to my body parts and to the trees and the grasses and the wild animals and the spirits.

Most of us sing and mutter gobbledygook to babies because this is the language infants understand and with them, we are unafraid to be foolish. How lucky we are to have children with whom we can feel free. How lucky we will be if we can feel free in the presence of each other—and with ourselves when we are alone—free to sing and wail and chant and babble. Free to love.

four

To Render Visible

Giving Birth to Images

"It does not matter how badly you paint so long as you don't paint badly like other people."
—GEORGE MOORE

"You are lost the instant you know what the result will be."
—JUAN GRIS

Drawing Blind

My mother, a firm believer in the higher education of women, enrolled me in kindergarten when I was four. Even though the southern California sun was ablaze in the November skies, the teacher had us participate in the sentiments of the season by fashioning snowmen. She handed out sheets of white paper which we were to tear into three circles of descending sizes and then paste together. My attempts at ripping paper into circles were hopeless. No matter how slowly I forced my fingers to move, my circles were not circles at all, but ovals and blobs. Nor could I make three shapes that had the correct relationship of decreasing sizes. My snowman had no proper parts: he would have an impossibly deformed bottom and a tilting midsection and a pinhead; or his middle would be as fat as his base, which would be square. He would be ugly, a complete failure, not unlike myself. A pile of discarded paper lay on the floor beside my desk, and my cheeks turned hotter and hotter as I stole looks around the room at my classmates' perfectly assembled works of rotund and jolly snowmen, complete with eyes and noses and horrifying happy smiles.

Finally, the recess bell rang and the room emptied. I stayed at my seat until I was absolutely sure that I was alone and, surreptitiously, I lifted the lid of my desk, slipped my hand into the dark chamber, and fumbled for my safety scissors. Holding the paper on my lap to avoid detection, I cut three jagged-edged circles of tapering sizes, doing my utmost to make them look torn. When the other students streamed back into the room, I was poring over my exemplary snowman in a contented trance, drawing black dots for eyes, a carrot for a nose, and a red arc for a smile.

The teacher walked up and down the rows of tiny wooden desks crooning over her students' artwork. She froze by my side—and then, with a movement swift as an eagle's descent on prey, she plucked my now beloved snowman from my desk, lifted him to her breast so that he faced the mob of staring kindergartners, and swooped him in a grand arc so that everyone could see as she squealed, "Nina cheated!"

I nearly wet my pants and had to squeeze deep inside my chest to hold back tears as the teacher laid my atrocity back down on my desk and continued her march through the aisles. On my way home, I ripped my snowman into shreds which I deposited in a neighbor's trash bin.

The majority of us have had experiences of being humiliated in our attempts to make art and, as a result, have abandoned all efforts. We leave art to the brave few who manage to sustain repeated insults to the ego and the psyche and survive as professionals in the land-mined field of creative self-expression. How absurd a sacrifice! Even if we make the most disgusting, ugly, stupid drawing the universe has beheld since the big bang, art making is still good for us.

In 1946, the British painter Edward Adamson opened an art studio at Netherne Hospital, a mental institution in the English countryside. At the time, mental institutions were fortresses in isolated locations with high iron-spiked walls and provided little in the way of treatment besides drugs, electroshock therapy, and mutilating brain surgery. Adamson, resolute in his belief that the process of painting created a direct dialog with the psyche, supplied materials and supported the residents in the making of art. He did not provide psychological analysis on the basis of the paintings and sculptures. Instead, he relied solely on the images themselves to restore balance in the mind.

"Where the problems of the mind are concerned," he writes in *Art as Healing,* "the solution must be found where they originated, that is, from within. It is here that we have the source of real change. Art obliges us to communicate with the inner self, and in so doing, to engage in a dialogue with both our destructive and creative forces. The destructive powers have precipitated the problem, so that the symptoms of illness we observe are merely the acting out of an unresolved, inward struggle. The gordian knot is much more effectively untied by the creative powers of healing Art, than cut by the surgeon's scalpel, or permanently concealed by tranquilizers."

The results of Adamson's experiment were remarkable—not only did the residents create bodies of gallery-worthy art, but they also experienced profound psychological transformation. Visitors often asked Adamson if he assisted the patients of Netherne with their art making. He did not, he replied, because his help was not needed. "The reason that the paintings are so positive in their statement is that they express the powerful creative energy that we all possess but may not have released," he maintains.

Most of us, whether or not we admit it to anyone within earshot, enjoy making art because, as Adamson points out, we make contact with the inner self. The inner self is not at all interested in the level of our talent, but only concerned that we engage and express. The ego, on the other hand, is acutely concerned about our level of expertise and stands in the way of our outpouring like a protective parent refusing to let a child do something deemed injurious: *I am protecting you from severe humiliation. Trust me. I know about these things. Let's face reality here, you are not an artist and you do not possess even a modicum of talent in that arena. Do not even think about picking up a paintbrush. Let me turn your attention to the truly vital tasks at hand, you have to dust the blinds, organize your sock drawer, color code every file folder, and pluck your eyebrows this instant.*

Despite the convincing nature of these arguments, the censoring mind is incorrect in its assessment of reality. Like "swimming or lovemaking, art is a behavior potentially available to everyone because all humans have the predisposition to do it," Adamson insists. Ellen Dissanayake in her book *Homo Aestheticus* presents another strong argument for the value of art making: ". . . art can be plausibly considered a biological need that we are predisposed to want to satisfy, whose fulfillment gives satisfaction and pleasure, and whose denial may be considered a vital deprivation."

To draw with ease, we must find a way to defuse the strategies of the censoring mind. Adamson observed that mental illness "can relieve some people of their inhibitions about painting." Fortunately, there are other ways besides having a nervous breakdown that can minimize the authority of the internalized censor. One is to draw with our eyes closed.

Drawing with the eyes closed allows us to create imagery without feeling responsible for what emerges, yet what emerges is a vital expression of our state of mind and heart. There is a primal longing in us to make art, a longing that remains enigmatic despite the heroic efforts of great intellects to understand the source and purpose of this impulse. We feel better when we make art. Why? We have explanations, but in truth, we do not yet fully understand the function of art making in human evolution and culture. What we do know is that the species has been making art for eons and that the act of art making, an activity some biologists hypothesize is actually encoded in our genetic structure, is essential to our psychological and physical health.

The Practice

Pull out a piece of drawing paper. Any paper will do, but it is useful to have a big piece of paper, 11" x 17" or larger. Gather a handful of your favorite drawing instruments: pastels, crayons, colored pens, charcoal, soft pencils. Or if you don't want to go to the trouble of collecting materials, grab any piece of paper within reach (a napkin, a receipt, the back of an envelope) and a pen or lipstick or burnt end of a matchstick. Sit at your desk, or kitchen table, or on the floor, or at a restaurant counter, or bus stop bench, or airport lounge with your paper and art supplies handy.

Close your eyes. Feel the surface of the paper with your hands, and its boundaries. *Without peeking,* draw with your eyes closed by letting the hand move freely on the paper, dictated by feeling and inner imagery. Perhaps you were up half the night in an amorous escapade and are sitting at your kitchen table still in your robe at noon. Let the feeling of delicious body sensations move your hand. Perhaps your plane was overbooked and you were bumped and have to wait for hours in the cramped holding area before heading for Tuscany. Allow the feelings of anger, disappointment, exhaustion be the energy that moves your hand. You do not need to *know* how you feel or name your emotions—anxiety, delight, apprehension—but only to let your current disposition direct the movement of your hand so that you by-pass the intellect. Instead of attempting to "draw" your feeling, let the feeling draw.

Work until you feel finished, take a deep, full breath, then open your eyes and look at what you've created. See without judgment—no *Yuk how disgusting, I hate my drawing, I hate myself, I hate this stupid book.* Take in the image, the shapes, the colors. The art will surprise you in some way. Receive that surprise.

Daily Portrait

For nine months, I was a resident artist at the Marin Headlands where, due to certain factors of enlightenment having struck the public-at-large, the military base had been converted to an arts center. My studio—a grand room with wooden floors, tall ceilings, rows of white columns, and a series of windows looking out onto the estuary—was in a former barracks at the end of a long road that wound its way through park lands. The only telephone in the immediate vicinity was a pay phone in a popular hallway of the building next door, so except for the other artists (who were enthusiastically admonished not to interrupt each other's hard-earned privacy) and the occasional intrepid tourist, I was far removed from the welcome distraction humans provide. I spent hours alone in my big room.

At work on a performance which was to open in a few short months, I didn't yet have a theme or a direction or a plan. I did have a newsprint pad and a set of colored pens you buy for children, which I intended to use to make charts about my show illustrating how the narrative elements intertwined, how the dynamics rose and fell.

One day, having danced and vocalized and talked to myself for an hour or two and still having no clue as to where I was headed, I sat on the floor and pulled out the pad and started drawing. Although I had enjoyed drawing since I was a child, I rarely engaged in the activity because I was not a visual artist but a performance artist. Honoring where my talent lay and where it did not, I applied myself to my chosen form and let the visual artists paint and draw. Suddenly incapable of tearing myself away from the pleasure provided by sixty felt-tip pens, I convinced myself that whatever I was doing was throwaway art, headed immediately for the bin. Free of the pressure to make something important, something that I might keep or show to anyone, I drew images without worrying about their merit in the real world of real art that had real value. Drawing was fun. And even though I was surrounded by authentic painters making art for downtown galleries and international festivals, and I was working on a performance and needed to figure everything out about it from scratch, I couldn't help myself, I kept drawing.

Each day, I made a self-portrait. Some days I spent only a few minutes at the task, other days I became more involved in the detail of the work, layering it with design and color. I was having a good time even though some of the drawings were not pleasing in the slightest. Since I had no intentions of becoming a visual artist (well, to be perfectly honest, perhaps I had secret longings that I refused to admit to the surface of consciousness), I could be horrid at drawing and still be happy doing it. The more I drew, the more engaged I became in image, color, and texture and the way inner feelings materialize in form. I began to see my life as if it were an animated cartoon, the story of a woman, day by day. Our lives may be difficult to endure, but generally, they make good raw material for the creating of art.

A woman crying blobs of crimson tears is wearing blue shoes and lying on a mountain peak.

A woman with doodles and spirals and squigglies inside her head is swimming in the waves.

A woman sleeps in the rain, naked, and you can see through her body to her bones.

Although the effect of self-portraiture might be therapeutic, the intention is not to make sense of the images, but to give the subconscious free access to manifestation without the need for evaluation, translation, or understood significance. Whether or not we comprehend the meaning of the images we create is irrelevant. The point is to make art without a need for results other than the art itself.

There is a grand paradox embedded in the process of all art making: to benefit most fully from the creative process, we must give up the need to benefit; we must surrender to the dictates of the process, not dictate to the process. Perhaps we draw a line and we see, clearly, that the line is unsatisfying alone and needs something. We *feel* this need, not intellectually, but in our bones, so we add another mark. If we attempt to interpret the meaning of the first line in order to add the next, we diminish the potential for the art to do its work on us. The therapeutic value of art making lies in the power of the subconscious having free rein as the eyes track the design that emerges, feeding information back to the subconscious so that a dialog is established. The more we are able to submit to the impulses of the inner being, the more enjoyable the process becomes, and the more authentic the product.

The psyche has mysterious ways of leading us to well-being. Our job is to allow the psyche to do its work—to follow the bidding of the creative impulse.

The Practice

Gather your materials: paper, pencils, crayons, water colors, felt-tip pens, or whatever is handy. If you're in a café, use a napkin; if you don't have a pen, borrow one from the waitress.

Draw a self-portrait. Perhaps you want to create a recognizable face or body: a head and a nose, eyes and lips, a torso with arms and legs. Perhaps you prefer to create an abstract work, letting line and color and shape be the expression of the moment. Add color, texture. The details can transform a work that is interesting into a work that is revealing.

Continue for as long as you feel interested. And then, go on for another minute or two. Often when we are unsure of how to proceed, we stop. But if we pause, and then continue, another element of design emerges, another visual episode. If we have the courage to proceed, we can deepen into the work and penetrate layers that are at first not available to our perception.

When you are finished, take a moment to look at your work without judgment. If we are able to regard our art without evaluating it, we can steep for a moment in the psyche's feeling of satisfaction for having emerged into the world of material form. This taking on of physical form is a delight to the inner self, allowing our subconscious to perceive its own existence.

Tack your drawing up on the wall or put it in a portfolio or stick it in your wallet so you can refer to it later. Even if you don't like your drawing, keep it and take a look at it in a few days or weeks with fresh eyes. Over time, you will detect the development of a personal vocabulary of imagery, a signature style. As you continue to practice, your work will take on a life of its own, becoming more significant to you and more satisfying.

When our emotions and experiences remain undercover and unexpressed, we tend to feel malaise—either as an underlying anxiety we are hardly aware of, or in a more overt way as a physical tic or an eating disorder or depression. As we express ourselves through images, the malaise often passes and in its wake, we feel more ease, more comfort, more happiness. And it is not only our anxiety and our fear and our disappointment and our rage that call for expression. We also have the need to express our contentment. We might draw ourselves dancing or making love or climbing a mountain or scuba diving. In giving attention to these moments of joy, we recall happiness and so cultivate well-being in our lives.

Thich Nhat Hanh has a following of Vietnamese refugees who experienced severe psychological trauma both during the Vietnam War and in the postwar era as boat people. In order to assist them in their psychological recovery, Thây (the name he is called by his students, pronounced "Tie") offers practices that give rise to states of calm and happiness. He explains that before we can successfully delve into our wounds, we must first stabilize the psyche through repeated experiences of well-being. To find the place of inner peace, we need access routes; once we know how to contact the core of tranquillity that resides within all of us, we can visit that place over and over again. To cultivate happiness, Thây teaches a meditation practice that involves smiling. He calls this mouth yoga: when the mouth is moved into a gentle smile, we feel better. But he does not rely on silent sitting practices alone; he also has his students write poetry, make flower arrangements, and sing together.

Studying with Thây for extended periods of time, I realized that the more I acknowledged even fleeting moments of contentment, the more extended my experiences of contentment became. Rather than simply hoping for happiness, we can actually develop it, the way one grows a flower in a garden by regular watering. And self-portraiture is one of the methodologies available to us to engender happiness.

Art That Abounds

I was walking one summer afternoon with my friend James along a country path in Germany that wound its way between villages through pastures and planted forests. James suddenly fell to his knees. I thought he was hurt.

"Careful," he whispered, and pointed to a leaf where a tiny dot of a bug had come to a halt. He reached for his Swiss Army knife, unfolded the miniature magnifying glass and handed it to me. I stared at a natural wonder: the bug's iridescent blue wings lay folded over its shiny black back, a yellow band shimmered around its neck, and red eyes popped from its pointed face.

We stayed on our knees for a long time, passing the glass back and forth until the tiny miracle crawled away.

"Amazing!" I said, and James smiled like a docent.

———————

Yesterday, I walked through a field where cows grazed and I settled onto a flat round of a bleached tree stump beside an estuary. The sun was shrouded by low clouds but still spread an even heat over the green meadow. I stretched out, closed my eyes, and dropped into a deep and welcome quiet, drifting in and out of awareness, my mind going soft and lazy in that close-to-sleep state that isn't quite napping but equally delectable.

Later, as I climbed back through the pasture, I noticed an animal moving in the distance, its markings resembling those of a cow, but its gait lithe and slinky. I pulled out my binoculars: a black-and-white cat was prowling through a pasture of black-and-white cows. I felt as though I was inside a Japanese painting, a Fellini movie, a visual joke, and I laughed out loud.

———————

"All you need to know comes in the moment before sleep," H. W. L. Poonja said over and over again during his morning talks in Lucknow. For days I had puzzled over his words. One morning during *satsang* (a group meeting with an enlightened master often consisting of dialog), I could hardly stay awake and found myself adrift in a calm, dark sea, Poonjaji's voice a hum in the distance. I kept forcing my eyes open in an effort to revive my attention, but to no avail; they fell shut and I found myself afloat again.

When *satsang* was over, I walked home down the dusty streets that bustled with rickshaws and three-wheeled taxis and meandering cows, and I chastised myself for having missed every word from the great master's mouth. Busy

with self-flagellation, I nearly overlooked what I, in fact, was perceiving—
everything around me had changed while remaining exactly the same. The
chant of the peanut boy sitting on his cart was as moving as a mother's lullaby.
A water buffalo with horns arcing skyward, his long brown face ending in a
soft spot of black nose, gave me a look as intimate as any lover's gaze. Even the
medallions of cow dung appeared to be emanating the esoteric perfection of
high art. I had touched an inner calm so healing that the world had transformed before my eyes, but the awakening I was experiencing was so mundane, I nearly missed it.

In that moment of deep rest, when all craving falls away, when we are un-
touched by ambition and fear and disappointment and hope, we find ourselves
in an impeccable silence that is always present at our core. For a moment, we
are free, and as we look around us all of life reveals its innate luminosity. But
for the mystery to stand revealed, we must be willing to pay attention to what
is right there before our noses, inviting us to pay attention even as we turn
away and gaze into the far distance, aching for what we believe is out of our
reach.

Walking along the road on the way back from the estuary yesterday, I leaned
over to study a white flower on a bush copious with blooms. Four paper-thin
petals with magenta dots at their bases surrounded a saffron yolk made of
hundreds of filaments. I pulled myself away and walked on.

As I rounded a bend, I noticed the shimmering green head of a mallard. I
had seen the duck swimming in the roadside pond on my walk out. *Just a mallard,* I had told myself and marched along. Now, as the duck paddled into a
turn, its emerald neck glinted as if struck by a spotlight and the power of the
color halted my movement. I felt like a female duck seduced by the potency
of this male's irresistible color. *It's just a mallard,* I told myself again, *nothing
rare or special; you can move along and get back to work.* But I couldn't move along.
Even though the duck was only a few yards away, I pulled out my binoculars
to get a more intimate look. A white stripe circled the base of his green

neck, and his beak, jutting from a dark face, was bright yellow. His beauty pierced me.

───

My friend Kathleen Harrison, who teaches botanical drawing, has her students observe a plant for several hours. She gauges the merit of their drawing not on the way the art looks, but on whether or not her students, throughout the hours of observation, have continued to notice details they did not originally perceive. Art is a way of seeing.

Everything is art, if we take the time to see. Not only nature's grand designs, but everything. I was walking in the streets of Soho one afternoon with Paul Zaloom, an artist who transforms found objects—rubber boots and broken umbrellas and discarded toy trucks—into animated objects that speak and interrelate in his performances. We passed a wooden crate jutting at an odd angle out of the gutter, the broken slats of pine as jagged as the Sawtooth Mountains. I knew that Paul had seen what I had seen: trash art. My perception had been influenced by Paul's way of seeing, without his having to say a word.

"The best thing about being an artist," Paul said, catching my thought, "is that you see art everywhere."

───

In the flurry of our busy lives, we rarely stop to notice the startling art that nature has sculpted. Yet by paying attention to what is present in our environment, we can experience the same lift of spirits we receive when going to an art gallery or taking a trip to the Grand Canyon. It is from these moments of wonder that creativity is sparked. Perhaps we draw a bug with a yellow neckband, or paint a yellow stripe around a teacup at a pottery-painting store, or pull out a dress with red polka dots we had tucked away in the back of the closet and go out dancing. The direct effect of an inspired moment of observation is often hard to track. Yet we know that when we are moved by seeing a great work of art, our sense of the visual aspect of the world is awakened and informs our entire state of being. When we feed our senses by observing the world with careful attention, art cannot help but emerge from us in one form or another. Inspiration finds its way through us into the universe.

One of the most profound acts of creation we can accomplish in our lifetimes is seeing clearly the art that abounds. Perception is a creative act—the art that surrounds us exists only when we become aware of it. The act of creation begins with the act of perception—they are inextricably intertwined.

The Practice

Look around. Notice the way light falls on an object close at hand. Notice the shape of a lamp or the pattern on a clock face or the curve of a cup's handle. Notice the relationship of one object to another. Notice color. Go outside, get on your knees, get close to something. Look carefully. Take time. Take as much time as you can bear looking at a flower or a leaf or a stone. Perception unfolds over time. When we become quiet, we see and, by seeing, we become quiet. The way grasses move is art. The way rain falls. The shape of a fence. The arc of a bird's flight. We live in an artful universe. God is an artist.

Don't worry about *making* anything from what you have seen. Let inspiration find its own way. We are training ourselves to see and from seeing, any number of creative acts are set into motion. Let the act of observation be your art making.

Impermanence

Okay, I tell myself, you're not in a very good mood so do something about it; make art. But no, I do not want to make art. I have no time and not even a molecule of desire to deal with staring at a blank page and making some mark

I am sure I won't like, so I decide instead to drink a cup of coffee even though I've just given up drinking coffee. I stare at the kettle and wait for the water to boil, the way my mother stared at the kettle when she was depressed and waited for the water to boil. And after I drink a strong brew of French roast, I am still in a bad mood and bad thoughts, propelled by caffeine, are running around my mind about how my thighs are drooping and my car didn't pass its smog check and I don't compost. Feeling worse than I did before I had the coffee, but having more energy, I say, "Okay, make art."

But no, I have not the slightest inclination to make art because what is the point, I need to get to work, real work, I need to mop the floors and find a place in my tiny yard for a compost pile, and anyway I don't want to look at anything I draw because I already know before having made anything that I will not like it, that in fact I will detest it. So I decide to make a sandwich, even though I'm not really hungry. I eat the sandwich, and the paper towel on which I have placed the sandwich—since I am too lazy to use a plate, and anyway why waste resources—is now blotched with mustard, and I pick up a pen that is lying alongside a pile of old mail, draw a loopy design around the mustard blob, and realize the marks look like petals. I know I am going to throw the paper towel away, so not even thinking about whether the flower I have inadvertently drawn is a good flower or an abominable flower because it is a flower headed for the trash, I draw a stem and leaves. I draw a pot for the flower, and add another flower to the pot, and dab a bit of extra mustard from my knife on the paper towel to make a center for the companion flower, and I realize I am liking my drawing, even though it is a stupid drawing. I like the way the ink has seeped into the nap of the paper towel and the way the mustard drop has been incorporated into the heart of the flower, and I think I am actually quite good at this, at transforming dirty paper towels into art, and that maybe I could start a new art movement.

Throw the paper towel away now, I tell myself, but I don't want to throw it away, I want to stick the art—which is now good art, important art, art that could launch my career as a visual artist with galleries in Chelsea and Paris—on the refrigerator behind a magnet; but the refrigerator magnets are already stretched to the capacity of their magnetism holding up photographs of my godchildren and brothers and nephews and nieces. So I throw the paper towel into the trash and, feeling much more optimistic about life in general, I proceed with my day.

———————

One of the four noble truths articulated in the teachings of the Buddha is that everything is impermanent. During long meditation retreats, you are told to focus on the reality of impermanence so you sit there on your pillow with your eyes closed and watch the breath come and go; and feel the tickle of fly feet on your cheek come and go; and listen to the sounds of someone breathing way too loud on the pillow next to yours come and go; and feel the pain in your knee come and go; and watch thoughts of when the bell will ring so you can get up and have a cup of strong tea with half-and-half and honey come and go until in a grand and terrifying epiphany you perceive all phenomenon arising and disappearing in tinier and tinier increments of time, nothing lasting, and you see how you and everyone you know is living in a universe of unstoppable, dizzying flux. This is supposed to be good for you, the teachers insist, but you are not sure why yet as you fall into a pool of tears struck with the now indelible realization that you and everyone you love are going to go to the great beyond regardless of how much you want to stick around in the company of your friends.

In monasteries, the monks and nuns chant the sutra on impermanence to continually remind themselves that nothing lasts and that clinging to any feeling or person or object of gratification results in suffering. I chant the sutra whenever I remember to, which is usually when I am in my car and prey to the arising of suffering due to a downturn in a romantic relationship or my career and I have already eaten chocolate and made an appointment to get a facial and am still in a horrid mood:

> *All things are impermanent*
> *They arise and they pass away*
> *To be in harmony with this truth*
> *brings great happiness.*

The chant works. I feel more calm despite the fact that the hillsides which were a lavish green only weeks ago have now turned brown; and my skin which was once perfect now has spots; and my hair is going gray at the temples; and I am starting to look like my mother, and will probably, horror of horrors, begin to resemble my grandmother if I have the great good fortune to live so long; and the bag of organic chocolate-covered almonds sitting on the car seat next to me is now completely empty.

The good news, I tell myself as I honk my car horn along with all the other drivers honking their car horns as we go through the tunnel toward the Golden Gate Bridge, is that not only does pleasure pass, but so does pain. And the even better news is that now having fully admitted the nature of reality to myself, I am noticing how uncommonly precious even this pain in the heart is, and as I emerge from the tunnel I see that the hills, which were once green and then brown, are now a pure gold ablaze in the glow of a setting sun.

Tibetan monks practice sand painting as a form of meditation. Using tiny metal cylinders, they sift bright-colored sand onto a board creating intricate designs of clouds and labyrinthine passageways and deities and elephants and snow-covered mountains. The creation of the mandala requires weeks of tedious work as the monks with their shaved heads and saffron robes bend over a large board and deposit sand in the thinnest of streams. But only days after completing the mandala, the monks, chanting mantras of dissolution, scrape the sand off the board—the forms dissolving, the colors running into each other in a pile of sparkling matter—and pour the sand into the ocean.

The object of the sand-painting practice is not to keep the artwork so that generations hence can admire the skill of the artisans, or to sell the artwork so that money can be raised, but to dissolve it so that the minds of the practitioners can detach from the product of their efforts and surrender to the uplifting freedom of flow.

All of us can make artwork that we know will disappear, art that we lay as offerings on the altar of impermanence. All of us can make art we intend for dissolution, returning dust to dust as we ourselves will return to dust; art that is a devotion to the truth of impermanence which when surrendered to becomes the very cause of our movement toward liberation.

When we develop the capacity to ride the waves of change, letting go of our need to have reality cooperate with our own wishes and instead wishing for an ability to be comfortable with reality as it presents itself, moment to moment, we discover within ourselves an abiding calm. No longer in a state of denial about the transitory nature of existence, we are able to celebrate this fleeting life before we, too, dissolve. We are able to cherish the pleasures life does provide not because we imagine they will last forever, but because we know they are temporary.

Andy Goldsworthy, the noted British artist, creates sculptures within the natural landscape out of leaves, stones, branches, icicles. His work is of extraordinary beauty. The visual elements are an integral part of the landscape they reside in and yet emerge as a distinct work of art separate from their environment. While the works are preserved through documentation—carefully produced color photographs assembled into books—the actual sculptures are temporary and it is in part the transient nature of Goldsworthy's art that makes the work so captivating.

One of the most pleasurable activities to do while outdoors is to make art. Temporary art. The materials we need are provided: leaves, sticks, branches, driftwood, pebbles, dirt, flowers, snow, sand. The landscape is free of critics except the ones who live inside our own minds. All we need to do is to pause, and play.

In order to build a sculpture outdoors, we find ourselves relating more intimately to our environment, seeing what we might have overlooked. We appreciate a shell or a colored leaf not only from a distance, but up close: we touch it, noticing heft and texture, color and design. Our own creativity becomes infused with the creativity of nature, our design and nature's design dissolving into each other.

The Practice

When you're on a hike or sitting in your backyard, on the beach, or even on your balcony if you live in the city, gather objects that call your attention and build an arrangement. You might place five white pebbles in a line on a large dark stone. You might put a red leaf in a bed of yellow leaves. You might put a single white seashell on a tiny piece of driftwood. You might take a fallen branch as a base and pile stones on top of it, sprinkle leaves like confetti over it, and crown it with feathers. Work without thinking or planning. Allow the part of your mind that enjoys shape and color to come forward and take over. Don't try to make sense of what you make, or judge your progress. Simply allow your hands to place things in relationship to one another.

When you are finished, look carefully at what you have created, then walk away. Continue your hike or your beachcombing, your picnic, or your jogging. Don't look back. Let your art go.

Found Object Art

I was invited one evening to attend a fund-raising soiree at the Pacific Heights home of an art-collecting couple. The presentation of the cause célèbre took place in the massive black marble foyer. Impressive works of contemporary art hung on the walls, lit perfectly with recessed pin lights. Only a few chairs were provided so most of the guests stood as an earnest woman talked at length about a terrible situation somewhere in the world that needed our attention. After a while, I became weary of standing and I propped myself on a ledge below the picture window looking out over the bay. Next to me sat a giant bag of kitty litter.

Later, when the talk was over and the schmoozing under way, the hostess took a small group of us on an art tour through the kitchen and hallways and bedrooms and offices and bathrooms. Not until I was putting on my coat and walking back out through the foyer did I realize the kitty litter was art—art that the couple had purchased from a reputable dealer, art that was masquerading as kitty litter, which in fact it was.

We can hold Marcel Duchamp responsible for this turn of events in contemporary art. Imagine the reaction of the art connoisseurs when he submitted a urinal to an exhibition in New York. Genius, some cried. The downfall of Western art, others bemoaned. In any event, Duchamp and the Dadaists changed the way we look at things, liberating art to the eyes of the beholder.

Duchamp was interested in creating work that would "combat logical reality," work that would not merely delight or intrigue the viewer because of the artist's mastery in representing landscape or figure, but that would transform perception itself. His experiments worked, and so we now have the liberty to regard any of the objects in our immediate environment—a bowl of paper clips, a half-eaten loaf of bread, a clock on a mantel—as art.

Found object art is about allowing the eyes to see art where ordinarily art is not recognized and to make art out of whatever we find, anywhere. Found object art is about chance, trusting that what is provided moment to moment in one's immediate environment has significance and therefore deserves to be noted. Found object art is a practice of devotion to ordinary things.

The Practice

Found object art is made by setting an object apart—by contextualizing it in a new way, by framing it, by placing it in a location, or in relationship to other objects, where it is seen rather than overlooked.

Find objects that attract you—a bowl, a discarded toy, a toothbrush—because of their shape or color or texture or statement about reality. You might find these objects in gutters, washed up on the beach, on your desk or your floor or in the cupboard. You can assemble them using glue or nails, scotch tape or knots, or balance and gravity. Or you can simply place objects in a setting where they will be noticed: five rolls of white toilet paper in a row on the back of the toilet tank; salt shaker sitting on a fig leaf in the middle of the kitchen table; matching soup cans on the mantel.

You can hang a found object: pink toothbrush on a bare white wall. Feature it on a pedestal: bag of dog kibble under a spotlight. Place it in the garden: statue of coat hangers. Build it in the corner of your desk: three red paper clips, one blue paper clip, three yellow paper clips. Hang it from a ceiling hook: wedding gown.

Found object art can be an instantaneous practice. When you feel the stirring to make art, or when you feel irritated or bored or angry, glance around your immediate environment and make art out of whatever you find. You can do this on the top of the filing cabinet, on the kitchen counter, on a restaurant table, on the dashboard of the car. Fork laid over knife in the center of a white plate. Pyramid of toothpicks. Shaving cream slash across a naked leg. Napkin framed by bread crumbs. Circle of fallen petals.

Most likely, you already make found object art. Sitting at a table with friends you move the cup and saucer around, or rip the napkin into pieces that you arrange on the plate. Now, knowing you are making art, that you are even part of an art movement, go ahead and elaborate, indulge, create.

While I was teaching a monthlong work-scholar program one winter at Esalen Institute, I had the opportunity to participate in a weekend workshop about relationships taught by a psychologist famous in the field of love. After a morning lecture, he had us spend the afternoon drawing a map of our relationship history from the time of our birth until the present day. We were to include everyone who had been important to us: parents, grandparents, siblings, best friends, stepparents, adolescent crushes, lovers, spouses, ex-spouses, molesters, children, stepchildren, pets. Working with pastels and colored pens on a large pad of newsprint, I fashioned lyrical curves and tortured twists, optimistic spirals followed by storms of black globs, orgasmic bursts and tormented eruptions, but by the end of the session, I felt I hadn't been able to truly evoke the essence of my relationship life and intended to continue the rendering when I had the time.

When I returned to my room, a small apartment a mile down Highway 1 where the work scholars are housed, I was greeted with the happy whines and lavish tail-wagging of my six-month-old cocker spaniel, Emma. In the middle of the floor lay a mass of dental floss, interwoven with Christmas tinsel, twigs, and brown strips of metallic audiotape. The plastic floss dispenser dangled from the middle of the two-foot arc of tangled waxed string. Emma's attempts at art seemed a far superior rendering of my relationship history than my own, so I tossed my work in the fireplace and saved hers, which now hangs on my bedroom wall. Guests, impressed with the sculpture, ask me who the artist is. Emma, I say. They go silent as they try to remember if Emma is a friend of mine they have met, the name so familiar—and then look at the art with new eyes as they realize I am referring to my dog.

By making art out of whatever we find, we kindle a quality of playfulness and we carry that spirit with us into our friendships and work relationships. We carry that spirit with us as we talk on the telephone and conjure marketing strategies and cook dinner and change diapers. Making art out of whatever we find, we desterilize our environments, we declassify our categories, we fall in love with chance, and we partner with our surround. Making art out of whatever we find, we change our lives—we combat logical reality and enter an artful universe that is made of salt shakers and Q-tips and urinals; a universe that invites us to join in the game of creation, now.

five

Words On Words

A Raid on the Inarticulate

"Truth is revealed. It cannot ever be told. It has to appear inside the telling or through the telling."
—James Hillman

Moving . . . On

One of the best acting teachers I have studied with, John Parkinson, had his students do hours of physical and vocal training before allowing them to use words. "The body comes first," he advised. "Let language come from the body." For an actor, vocal and physical presence are central to her craft, but it is not actors alone who rely on their bodies for self-expression—we all do. While we might write a short story or a poem without ever dancing or singing, the quality of the short story or poem is likely to be enhanced if we were to dance and sing for a minute before, or during, our periods of writing. If the body is tense, the mind tends to also be constricted.

I have a novelist friend whose sentences are tightly knit commentaries on the human condition. They spin from a particular detail of a character's behavior into the deep regions of the psyche and back without a spare word, and he is likely to spend half a day crafting a single paragraph. In the process of working in this scrimshaw style, his mind can become contracted, so he plays music and dances wildly around his room for as long as it takes to free up his physical energy and loosen the mental bind. Then he goes back to writing.

If you have been following the exercises in this book, you will by now have danced for at least a minute, and babbled with your voice for at least a minute, so we can move on to the question of writing. But remember, when you write, take a break now and then to move, to scat, to doodle, to sing.

Love and Language

One of the many delights of writing is that as we jot down our thoughts and feelings and experiences, we discover what we think and feel and know.

Humans are paradoxical—we appear to be the only animals who are self-reflective, and yet we are often unaware of the layered contents of our own hearts and minds. Unaware of this unawareness, we proceed blissfully (or miserably) as unacknowledged internal dynamics steer us through our activities and influence the choices we make moment to moment to moment. More often than not, much of what we are experiencing escapes us until we engage in practices that reveal what lies submerged. So we write—we write to allow what is inside of us, lurking, bubbling, churning, to emerge and be seen. As our experience is given form on the page, insights and syntheses arise. We write to make sense of our lives, and when our lives refuse to make sense, we write to befriend the chaos.

My neighbors' daughter, Jessamyn, turned two yesterday. I gave her a gift that she opened with the particular glee of a toddler still new to the experience of birthdays. She pulled a stuffed monkey from its shroud of tissue paper and pointed to its nose.

"Nose," she said, and her parents and I repeated, "Nose," and we looked at each other and grinned—what intelligence, what a vocabulary, what a thrill—and Jessamyn, seeing our glee, pointed at the dark beads of monkey eyes and said, "Eyes," and waited for us to respond, which we did instantly. We laughed out loud; and then she laughed out loud and we could hardly stand how much fun we were having.

"Ear," Jessamyn said. And we howled.

Human beings love language: spoken words, written words, stories, poems, songs. Language is a craving that seems to be encoded within our genetic structure. As infants, we gurgle with sounds, our tongues and lips eager to form voiced communication. We learn to print our names—the letters misshapen and backward, transgressing the blue lines within which we have been instructed to remain—which we present with pride to parents and grandparents who oooh and ahhh, and then post our barely legible signatures on refrigerator doors for daily reverence. Next, we are forced to stand in front of our peers and, as anxiety flushes our faces, spell words out loud one treacherous letter at a time, words whose sounds barely resemble the units that compose them: xylophone, incandescent, porphyry. Then we are made to slog our way through the classics, our progress waylaid by the search through onion-thin pages of massive dictionaries for definitions of words we have never seen before and might never manage to incorporate into our spoken vocabularies: castellan, scammony, isochronous. In rebellion, we make up words of our own and new ways to use old words: bad, cool, dis, dude, da bomb. And finally, having survived the journey of words into adulthood, we have our own children and read them bedtime stories and admire their barely legible scrawls and coach them through spelling bees as we croon with delight over each development of their skills, generation after generation after generation.

Through our use of language, culture arises and transforms. By codifying our experience and our understanding into words, we are able to arrive at knowledge built on the assembled parts of the collective, and civilization rushes forward through time, colonizing new frontiers: the minutiae of quantum particles, the unfathomable regions of space, the interior of the human mind.

But however useful, language suffers unfortunate limitations. In and of itself, the symbols we have created to communicate meaning, mean nothing. We confer significance consensually; meaning lives not in the word but in the act of bestowal. So the craft of the writer is to use language in a way that most effectively inspires the granting of meaning by the one who reads. Even if the only one to read the writing is the writer herself, the process is the same—a meeting between subconscious and conscious layers of the mind, emerging first as thought forms, which are then translated into symbolic language on paper, and finally reconstituted as meaning in the mind of the reader. Magic.

The writer, conjuring images through words, is a sorcerer whose tricks bear fruit in the imagination of the reader. And because we are human, we are deeply enamored of this process. As we learn to use language in a way that expresses our thoughts, feelings, and experiences more and more clearly, more and more poetically, more and more precisely, we fall more deeply in love with language and with our lives.

Writing Guidelines

Regardless of whether we are writing only for the personal experience of the process, or if we are writing with the intention of crafting a piece worthy of publication, the same guidelines prevail:

1. While we are writing, the work will benefit if we imagine we are writing for our own eyes only. Like going into a room, drawing the curtains closed, and locking the door so that in a moment of protected privacy we can experience ourselves unobserved, writing in a journal that no one will ever read is a way we can expose aspects of ourselves we tend to keep hidden. When we write, we discover and reveal what is shrouded; we make connections, we arrive at a deeper wisdom about ourselves, our relationships, and the world we inhabit. While we write, we cultivate clarity of mind. Writing is a meditation, a devotion, a solitary occupation.

2. Keep the hand moving. Natalie Goldberg, in her excellent books on writing as spiritual practice, instructs us to allow the flow of the subconscious to emerge through the moving hand. If we wait to refine our insights and craft our language, we allow an opening for the censoring mind to invade our thoughts and impede our access to subconscious imagery. Instead of being careful and precise, let the words flow from the fingers unencumbered. We can return to a piece of work if we are drawn to it, and rewrite. Or we can choose at times to write slowly, carefully, with great precision. But to discover what lies within us, beyond the realm of our approval or disapproval, to discover the truth, we must give ourselves permission to allow the rush and to let the hand move as quickly as the mind is moving.

3. Rather than needing to know the outcome of the piece before you begin—the beginning and middle and end of the story—let one word lead to the next. Don't know. Don't plan. By relaxing into the moment-to-moment arising of impulse, image, and language, we allow an inner knowing to emerge. Our minds are infinitely more intelligent than we realize, and the only way to tap into this innate understanding is to surrender control. If we

are working on a piece for publication, or a screenplay or stage play, then an outline or plot or character study might be very useful. But as we embark on the writing, we need to allow a freedom to emerge within the framework of the structure.

4.   Take time. Five minutes or ten minutes or twenty or an hour. During this allotted period, arrange all of your necessities within reach—a cup of tea, a pen, paper, your computer, Kleenex, a lit candle, a spritz of aromatherapy, whatever it is you might need and then—WRITE.

5.   As you write, you might begin to feel uncomfortable, antsy, anguished, exhausted. Often discomfort arises when we begin to work with material that is of profound significance in our lives and might reveal aspects of our being we tend to repress. If discomfort arises, stick with the process, keep writing. Welcome the pain. Write about the anxiety. Our best material is often the very experience we do not want to write about, the experience we refuse to express. Allow yourself to go into forbidden territory and explore as far as you are able. Write what you do not want to write. Write what you believe is of interest to no one. Write what you cannot tell your closest friend or your spouse or your child or your partner. You do not need to show this work to anyone. You can burn the pages. You can lock them in a file cabinet in an unmarked envelope. You can put them in the safe. Or on the altar.

6.   Conversely, write about nothing. Rather than writing about an issue you know is important, write about something mundane. Let the ordinary lead you into significance. Everything is meaningful. The mug you bought in Chinatown. The pencil with the name of a car wash in gold print. The postcard from a friend in Heidelberg.

7.   Be irreverent. Often we are able to laugh at events we considered quite excruciating when we experienced them but now, upon reflection, the same events resonate with irony and humor. Honor irony and humor.

8.   Lynn Freed, a novelist with whom I have studied, teaches many guidelines, but my favorite is "The only rule is what works." If what you are writing works on the page, the guidelines are irrelevant. Make up your own rules. Break all of them if you please, systematically, one by one, or simultaneously in a single paragraph. Transgress. Invent. Frolic. The only rule is what works.

Details on Details

When telling a story the most important guideline I have run across, besides "what works," is "Use details." Life isn't generic, it comes in particulars—colors, textures, smells, tastes, sounds, qualities of light, sensations. I'm not simply sitting at my desk; I'm sitting on an ergonomic chair I bought from my friend Sally. The chair has a number of levers and knobs, which Sally explained I was to adjust every hour, shifting my sitting position for optimal health of spine and ligament; but I ignore the options and find myself perched on the end of the blue padded chair, my back free of the support I spent a fortune on.

We want to be perceived as important people with profound ideas. But when we try to be profound, our writing can become didactic and pompous. If we look carefully, we see that the way we arrived at our theories about life and love, science and the stock market, health and religion, child rearing and rose gardening, was through living. We synthesized information from specific experiences that we codified into theories. Readers are interested in sharing a lived experience and being guided through this experience to whatever insights the author might have gleaned, rather than being told only the writer's conclusions about life in general. I am not recommending that we avoid speaking about what is important and profound—I am recommending that we tell the facts because that is where truth lies hidden.

Stories and the images they are made of are what move us and stick in our memories. Stories and the images they are made of are the means by which we come to understand our lives. How did my grandmother cook fish? How did my father comb his thinning hair? What kind of undershirt did my lover wear when I first saw him undress? In what book did he stash the postcard from the woman he was having an affair with and on what page? Stories, and lives, are made from particularities.

In contemporary culture, particularly in the West, we are trained to develop our critical faculties. If someone writes, "My boyfriend Bob is cruel," we might think in an instant (without even realizing we are thinking these thoughts because they are so quick and automatic), *Oh, that's interesting, but maybe what you mean by cruel isn't what I mean, or maybe you did something that ag-gravated him and he was cruel in response.* But if the same author writes, "I met Bob when he was working as a naturalist in the rainforest. On our last night in the jungle, he took me out alone to show me a tarantula. He poked the end of a branch into a hole in the ground and the creature emerged, big as a baseball with hairy legs. I emitted a muffled scream, even though I am not usually afraid of spiders. 'Wait here,' Bob whispered and disappeared into the dark-ness that throbbed with the chanting of insects. He came back with a cicada cupped in his hand, plucked off its wings, and tossed it down the tarantula hole. The injured insect screamed as it tumbled, the echoing howl amplified by the tunnel walls—until a moment of terrible silence. 'Great sound, huh?' Bob asked, a big grin on his face. 'Want me to get another one?' "

Here, we are reading the author's experience, not her treatise on cruelty. We are being told what happened, and from that information we are allowed to make our own assessments about Bob.

Details draw us into a story, generalizations tend to push us away. But that's a generalization, and like all generalizations, it is only true some of the time. A skilled writer might choose to compose an entire story using only generalizations to achieve a particular effect. But, for the most part, the de-tails of a life reveal the truth within a story. A narrative might contain a sprin-kling of theories for flavor, emphasis, intellectual satisfaction—but these theories are most effective when they rest on a foundation of details.

The Practice

Close your eyes and get quiet. When you open your eyes, let your gaze fall on a particular item in your environment: a glass, a pencil holder, a tree, a clock. Write about that object, using details. Don't worry about being meaningful or profound; let the object lead you into the intimacy of its being.

> Why are you doing this, writing about a clock or a pen or a paper clip? To practice focusing on details. To learn to value the particular. We tend to speak in generalizations and incorporate psychological jargon into our conversations. "I think I'm developing an eating disorder." But as a writer, reporting ideas isn't enough—the reader wants to know how the dill pickle slipped through your fingers which were already sticky from the chocolate bar with almonds you bought at the 7-Eleven at midnight.

Our art, and our lives, are transformed by our awareness. As awareness of the particularity of our lives becomes more precise, more clear, our understanding deepens—and out of understanding, wisdom arises.

To Know Things Intimately

And so each venture
Is a new beginning, a raid on the inarticulate

T. S. ELIOT

I am at my studio at the Headlands Center for the Arts. The sun, shining through the skylight, casts a glow across the canted ceiling. I study the band of light on the rough grain of wood and I search for language to describe the feeling that is evoked by this light. I am only able to find clichés: peace, radiance. These words do not accurately describe the experience I am having by looking closely at a glowing beam, so I abandon my search for language and instead direct my attention to *feeling* my experience—and I linger there, in the realm of sensed reality that refuses to be reduced to words.

Experience cannot be truly captured by language, only evoked. The task of the writer then, is to elicit a feeling in the reader—to provide enough sense detail that the reader can *enter* the scene and be transported from his place outside the story to reside within the story, be it a bedroom in Manhattan, a mountain trail in Guatemala, the front seat of a car on a French country lane, or the mind of a suicidal character. Words are a meager means of evocation. Our experience is too multifactorial, too synesthetic, too complex, to ever be spoken. But we can point. We can invite. We can cajole, surprise, evince, and summon.

The writer cannot evoke an experience if she does not cast the light of attention on her own moment-to-moment thoughts, perceptions, and sensations. The work of the writer, then, is not only to wordsmith, but to experience life fully enough, with enough awareness, that what she elicits in the imagination of the reader resonates with truth—not theoretical meaning, constructed meaning, but the raw and unadulterated feeling of life itself. The sun on the beam is significant because it glows, because the time is late afternoon, because the skies are not cloudy but clear, because light in winter, angled light, is weak and welcomed, and because there are white caps on the dark blue of the ocean and the month is January and the wind which makes its way through the cracks in the walls is cold.

We can err on the side of using too many details so that the heart of a narrative is obscured rather than revealed, but more commonly, even after being nudged to incorporate particulars, we avoid the use of details in order to get to the point of the story, which is usually a strong emotional experience or a meaningful theory about an experience. We do not trust that the details are where reality exists, where meaning exists. "God lives in the details," said Mies van der Rohe, but we look for God elsewhere.

We know life through our senses: smell, touch, taste, sight, hearing. And each of these senses delivers particulars. We do not see an apple, we see a red apple with a bruise on its skin near the stem and a small blue label with yellow print that says "organic." We don't smell cooking, we smell onions or curry or chocolate or cinnamon.

By exploring what we are experiencing, we become aware of the actuality of that experience. We develop the skill to perceive what is going on right now. When we come to have a felt relationship with the reality of the present moment, our lives, and our art, resound with richness, depth, wisdom; not because we have an opinion about things, but because we have come to know things intimately.

The Practice

Close your eyes. Notice smells. Before naming the aromas you detect, pay attention to the smells on a preverbal level. Open your eyes and describe what you are smelling. You can make a list of words: *onion, vanilla, sour, seaweed, cigarette smoke, jasmine.* Or you can make phrases: *the leather jacket hanging on the back of the kitchen chair; the dog still wet from her afternoon walk; the lamp light, a burning smell, the smell of heat.*

We have a very limited vocabulary for smells so describing them can be quite challenging. Yet, unless we have lost our sense of smell, aromas are a part of our moment-to-moment experience of life. If I have the capacity to describe my experience to you, you will be able to enter that experience and so come to know my reality as I come to know it myself.

Close your eyes and feel the sensations in your head and arms and legs and belly and back and neck. In your muscles, your organs, on your skin. Take your time. A particular sensation might intrigue you. Feel it. Examine it. Pain can be sharp or dull, throbbing or steady, located in one area or diffused. Warmth can be evenly felt or more intense in the feet or the hands. Pay careful attention. Open your eyes and write what you feel: *a tightness spreading between my shoulder blades like a strap; a burning in my eyes; my upper lip, the left half curling with a hint of tension and effort.*

Close your eyes and listen. Some sounds, like a passing car, might come and go quickly; others—the refrigerator humming, the television, the heater or air conditioner or a neighbor's radio—might be steady but have fluctuations within the steadiness. Listen carefully. Write down what you hear.

Close you eyes. Can you sense taste in your mouth? Bitterness, sweetness, sourness, moistness. Take a bite of something and pay attention to taste. Taste is affected by texture, by temperature. Write down what you notice.

What are you seeing? Let the eyes fall anywhere. Notice color, shape, form, texture, shadow, light. Look carefully. Write down what you see.

If you don't have much time, pick one sense door and write for a minute or two. If you don't want to take the time to write, simply notice what you are smelling, hearing, tasting, feeling, seeing. You can do this exercise anywhere. While on the subway or a bus or while driving. While walking or talking on the telephone or drinking tea. We often find ourselves waiting: on hold on the telephone or on line at the ATM. Use this time to notice the information rushing through the doors of perception. You will benefit from the effects of this practice whenever you do take the time to write.

Associating from Detail

Often we don't write because we can't decide what it is we might want to write about. We feel we can only begin when we know what we are going to say. As with the processes I have described in the previous chapters—processes of movement, visual art, and vocalizing—we can embark without knowing where we are headed, without having even the vaguest idea of what will emerge from our creative efforts. All we need do is begin, and then continue, allowing one word to follow another. But knowing this does not help us get started. So how do we begin?

I was commissioned to give a performance last year at a conference on retirement sponsored by the University of California. One of my fellow presenters was a neurologist, well into her seventies, who continued to teach and conduct research on brain function. She told us that dendrites, branches of nerves in the brain which are partly responsible for our intelligence, continue to grow as we age if we exercise the mind by learning new physical skills and broadening our intellectual knowledge. When we stop learning, our brains stop growing dendrites and we lose mental acuity. Associative thinking is particularly effective in stimulating the growth of dendrites, she had discovered through extensive research. The more our minds work associatively, leaping from one subject to the next in a pattern defined by tangents rather than lines, the more intelligent we become.

Not only does associative thinking augment our intelligence as we age, but working with associative processes also gives access to images that feed our art and provide a launching pad. By exercising our associative skills, we can learn to let inspiration spring from anything: a pink rose, a pile of driftwood, a park bench. We can use associative processes to jettison us into a "free write," and grow dendrites at the same time.

The Practice

Make a list of images that you see or hear or smell or feel in the immediate environment:

> The gold rim around the dinner plate
> A purple candle, scented with lavender
> A black case for eyeglasses
> The teakettle hissing.

Now, go back and add the words "reminds me of" to the end of each phrase, and finish the sentence:

The gold rim around the dinner plate reminds me of Emily's wedding ring.

A purple candle scented with lavender reminds me of the summer during the drought when I harvested lavender from Su and Mel's garden.

A black case for eyeglasses reminds me that I got a postcard last week from my ophthalmologist reminding me a year had passed since my last exam.

The teakettle whistling reminds me of the sound of wind in the forest of longleaf pine.

Continue this practice for a few minutes, associating from as many elements in your immediate environment as possible. The associations can be literal, as above, or more abstract:

The palm tree reminds me of salsa dancing.

The brick patio reminds me of my uncle who builds shopping malls.

The wastebasket reminds me of e-mail petitions.

Work as quickly as you can, without thinking. Make sense—*the clock reminds me of the fifty-yard dash when I was eleven; the lamp reminds me of suntans.* And don't make sense—*the green mug reminds me of horses; the Zip drive reminds me of freeways.* Free the mind.

As we associate from ordinary objects, we gain access to the stories that lie in the subconscious but are hidden from our intellect, which is why many schools of modern psychology rely on associative processes as a way to discover the dynamics of a patient's inner world that directly influence his outer behavior. Once these inner images are revealed, we are able to see our lives more clearly, and we feel better. But it is not only our inner dynamics that become revealed. As we free the mind to associate from the ordinary images that populate our environment, we actually change the way we see the world.

Mountains, coffee cups, lampshades, pencil holders, dulled by the habitual ways we perceive them, are suddenly seen anew. Ordinary reality regains a quality of mystery and richness. The pencil holder reminds me of a camel safari in Rajasthan. The skylight reminds me of the cave I slept in on Crete. The yellow Post-it reminds me of petals falling from tulips.

Let the Hand Move

So we have this list of images we've associated from other images; now what? Pick one and write. Just write, letting the hand move on the page. Let go.

Let go of what? Of control, of effort, of judging, of worrying, of concepts about how your life should be, of concepts of how your writing should be, of what you want, of what you don't want, of victimization, of fear. One word will lead to the next, one phrase unfold after the one before, sentences will bound across the page, paragraphs accumulate, if you allow the mind to relax and the hand to keep moving. But if you evaluate the work as you write, you will stop yourself midstream. You can evaluate the work later, after you have allowed yourself to spew on the page.

Often I have the experience during a free write of feeling as though what I am writing is complete drivel, and I can't believe I am such a vapid human being. The only way I can continue is to promise myself that I will stuff the crappy paragraphs of insipid nothing in a shredder. But when I finish and I read the piece, I discover meaning revealed in the narrative that would not have been bared had I tried to figure things out beforehand and attempted to write marvelous sentences with perfect verbs and stunning metaphors. And in fact, when I read what I have written, I often find some very tasty verbs and metaphors. I realize, too, that having written, my mood has improved. Something within my psyche has snaked its way out and does not care a jot if my sentences are worthy of publication or headed for the recycling basket.

For the duration of a free write, surrender to the flow of words and witness rather than control the emergent narrative. See what happens if you stop censoring.

The Practice

Choose one of the associations from your list that you developed in the previous practice, and write a narrative.

The gold rim around the dinner plate reminds me of Emily's wedding ring, you might begin. But where do you go from there?

Ask yourself where you are.

We were standing in her garden.

Ask yourself what you are doing in this scene.

Emily and Paul had asked me to marry them, to be the officiant.

What are you wearing?

What are you seeing?

What are you hearing?

What is the temperature?

Avoid telling us how you feel. Instead let the details reveal whatever emotions are arising:

The sun was hot, shining on the small gathering of family members who clustered under Chinese paper umbrellas and used their programs for fans. I realized I was smiling at the couple, who stood facing me. I had tucked a Kleenex into my sleeve (just in case I would be moved the way I usually am at weddings, in that weird poignant way, and I end up with mascara painting rivers down my cheeks) but now, I wasn't worried at all about mascara because I was worried about saying the right words. This was the first wedding I had ever conducted. Emily, on the other hand, was a fountain of tears. "I do," she said, her mouth wet, eyes red, and knowing she would be crying, she had not even bothered to wear makeup at all.

She was also smiling, that kind of smile that insists on taking over the lips,
that has nothing to do with being polite or appropriate, that conquers the
face. And I did the "I now pronounce you" part and Paul kissed Emily full
on the lips and everyone threw birdseed at the now officially married, by
me, couple.

Twenty-four Hours

If your everyday life seems poor, don't blame it, blame yourself; because for
the creator there is no poverty and no poor, indifferent place.

RAINER MARIA RILKE

If our lives appear impoverished, the fault lies not in our lives but in our lack
of awareness. Looking more deeply, however, we come to understand that we
cannot blame our awareness alone, for it is not awareness that is at fault, but
the constraints we have placed on expression. Once given an outlet, our
awareness rewards us with a glimpse into its rich storehouse of images, memories, dreams, thoughts, and feelings.

I improvise on a regular basis with my performance partner, Corey Fischer. After spending a solid hour warming up, we each do a ten-minute solo
improvisation while the other witnesses. Often when I walk out onto the
floor, I feel a panic rising as I scan my life in search of some meaningful material and find nothing worthy of utterance. No matter how often I have found
material hidden in the most banal of events, I am convinced that now my life
is truly bereft of any significance.

I begin with a movement and I allow the movement to lead me into language. Inevitably what arises appears too mundane and at first, I refuse the
image. But the image persists and I allow myself to describe it. I see my garden, a trowel nose-down in the patch where the tomato plants have gone
brown because it is winter. So I say, "The trowel is nose-down in the earth

where the tomato plants have gone brown." I do not know what I will say next because in and of itself, the trowel means nothing to me. But then I remember that the trowel was given to me by a friend for my birthday in a wooden box. And so I talk about the trowel in the wooden box and my friend with prematurely white hair. I remember that my grandmother had red rosebushes lining the walkway to her front yard and geraniums along the side of her house, which she watered each evening with a green hose. I remember that my gardener, who has long black hair, has been in Vermont with her sister who is dying from breast cancer. I could go on and on. But I do not go on and on, I work for ten minutes, and within the time frame, a story takes shape with a beginning and a middle and an end, and within the story I find my life rich with meaning.

A practice I give to my students is to write about something that has occurred in the past twenty-four hours. I encourage my students not to know which event or cluster of events they will write about before they begin, but to start with a single image and go from there. When they become confident about their ability to find material from the last twenty-four hours, I tell them to write about an event that occurred in the past twelve hours. Again, I encourage them not to premeditate, but to begin with a single image and let one image lead to the next. Now write about something from the last two hours, I say, and they groan but do it anyway. And finally, they write about the last ten minutes. What we discover is, contrary to having nothing to say, we have enough material to last for multiple lifetimes.

The Practice

Close your eyes and breathe for a moment and relax. Then, scan the past twenty-four hours of your life as if you were watching a movie. Notice which experiences, now that you are taking the time to pay attention, hold some charge for you. Some incident might pop up that you overlooked: seeing a dog run across the road unattended, or being struck by the beauty of a flower arrangement in the foyer of a restaurant, or noticing the hairs on the back of a man's hand. Or an incident might come to mind that is clearly significant and now you can take the time to explore it: rear-ending a red Jaguar, your child losing her first tooth, cutting your finger while you chopped mushrooms. Notice details as you scan: the kind of sheets on your bed, the crumbs on the floor of your car, the color of your toothbrush.

Let the mind land on a single image from the last twenty-four hours and begin to write. You can start with squirting a dollop of rosemary shampoo in the palm of your hand, or putting on brown socks, or listening to "Fresh Air" while you inched along in traffic. You may not have even the vaguest inkling of the meaning this image holds— write anyway. Or, if some particularly profound experience occurred, you may have a strong sense of the significance. No matter. Trust whatever arises and write it down. Often we end up addressing concerns that were not immediately apparent during the experience itself. The gift writing provides is a method for discovery.

Decide before you begin how long you will write, twenty minutes or fifteen or ten, or two, and then continue for the length of time you have set for yourself.

It is important to be disciplined at the beginning of the exercise and pay little mind to the voices that insist you have absolutely nothing to write of any value at all; if you make it through the gateway guarded by these demons, you will find yourself in the midst of a fountain of interesting material and see your own life with renewed vision.

When we pay attention and give expression to the richness inherent in our lives, we are in turn rewarded with rich lives.

Finding the Rub

A theory I've heard (attributed to Lily Tomlin) says that language was invented because people needed to complain. We long to kvetch about back pain and spouses having affairs and aging parents and lawyers' fees and taxes and global warming and traffic and adolescents and hard-disk crashes and root canals and the housing market and poverty and hunger and doctors and the weather. I am now going to provide you an opportunity to complain for a good reason; to complain for the benefit of your art; to lift complaint to lofty heights of spiritual self-expression. But there are rules to follow. Do not write about the theories you have about all and everything. Stick to the facts and write sentences abundant with juicy details.

The Practice

Identify what's bugging you right now. Your neck hurts. A cop needing to meet his quota pulled you over and issued you a speeding ticket when you were driving in a perfectly safe manner, and now you have to go to traffic school. Stepping out of the shower, you glanced in the mirror and noticed your thighs were sagging and clumped with cellulite and you can never wear shorts again. Your friend is in her sixth week of chemotherapy and has lost all of her hair and spent last night hovered over the toilet vomiting. You were sitting in your soft chair last night eating soba noodles and tofu while watching the news, and the newscaster announced that the president is making plans to drill for oil in pristine wilderness regions, and you couldn't finish your dinner so you threw your chopsticks at the screen.

Write away. Use details. Avoid theory and judgment and opinion. Do not use phrases like: I hate it that . . . I love it that . . . I can't stand . . . I believe in . . . I long for . . . I am happy when . . . I am sad because . . .

We do not care about your feelings, I tell my students who have usually done lots of psychotherapy and relish expressing emotions with great vigor. But no matter how many times I remind them to ground emotions in contexts and characters, someone bursts into tears on stage and tells me how sad she is about life in general. "What did you eat for breakfast?" I ask and she says, lips trembling, "A smoothie with orange juice and a banana and protein powder and two heaping tablespoons of spirulina and I didn't put the lid on the blender tightly enough and it splattered all over the kitchen." At which point we become interested.

"What were you wearing?" I ask.

"A T-shirt with 'Female Perversions' printed on it and my ex-boyfriend's boxer shorts that he left in my laundry basket when he moved out that were now covered in wet green spots."

Now we are even more interested in this woman's life because we can taste it and smell it and see it.

You can go ahead and express emotion, but do it through the details and the facts. The way a person lifts their hands from the steering wheel, or watches a child playing in the sand, or smells jasmine can reveal if the person is ecstatic or depressed, hopeful or disheartened.

Stick to the facts.

Singing My Mother to Sleep

We tend to see life from only our own vantage point, which is conditioned by our time in history, the place where we live, the culture we are a part of, the culture of our ancestors, our religion by heritage, our religion by choice, our gender, our sexual preference, our age, our personal desires and needs.

Often, no matter how correct or truthful our take on things is, it is limited. Real truth is not limited. Real truth is panoramic and sees reality from all angles at once.

In 1984, I made a performance work called "Singing My Mother to Sleep." I had been commissioned to do a piece at a gallery in San Francisco and, for weeks, I went to my studio in the flats of Berkeley and improvised, searching for material, unable to decipher a coherent theme. My dreams however, were annoying in their consistency—night after night I had nightmares of missing my mother's funeral. I would be in my Volkswagen Bug, lost on sinuous streets in the hills, and by the time I arrived at the cemetery, the guests would be leaving. Or in the dream I would wake up and realize the funeral had been the day before. And then I would really wake up and remember the funeral had been years ago and that I had not missed my mother's funeral, but had organized the entire proceeding. I had selected the coffin at the Jewish funeral home on Geary Street; met with the rabbi to fill him in on the details of my mother's life; ordered bouquets of red carnations, her favorite flower; written the obituary with the funeral director; chosen the chartreuse suit of crinkled silk for her to wear during her passage to the netherworld; made my way to the dais during the service to say what a good mother she had been.

But she had not been a good mother. She had been a difficult mother; a mother who loathed cooking and cleaning and rarely indulged in such domestic activities; a mother who spent most of her days in bed; a mother who hired taxicab drivers to follow me when I went on dates and report back to her the details of my behavior; a mother who had tape recorded my telephone conversations to use as evidence against me.

Even so, I grieved. For a year, I found myself bursting into tears at unexpected moments: as I reached for detergent in the aisle of a supermarket; as I braked for a red light; as I swam across a lake the way she had, with a strong and steady stroke that didn't tire. After a year, the pain lessened, and after two years, faded even more. So why, seven years later, was I having nightmares?

I pulled out a file folder of her papers that I had saved, but not read, and finally studied the handwritten pile of letters and poems and notes. Encoded in this small collection of personal papers, I discovered a story of my mother's life that until then I had not known.

My mother had been enrolled in a doctoral program at Stanford University and was writing a thesis about how young girls aspired toward servile professions (stewardess, waitress, nurse) while boys aimed at more authoritative jobs (pilot, doctor, lawyer). These patterns of aspiration, she maintained, were introduced the moment a child entered public school. In the 1950s, my mother was dedicated to transforming the educational system so that girls would aim for and feel confident in achieving the highest of professional goals. In 1955, the year that her father died and my father remarried a woman twenty years his junior, my mother failed her oral exams. Crushed, she took to her bed and emerged only for occasional professional meetings and to head for the malls. She shoplifted. She was arrested. Her teaching credential was rescinded. She spent even longer hours in bed until late afternoon when she went off and rarely returned before midnight. To this day, I have no idea how she spent the hours. Bars? Movie theaters? Malls? Bowling alleys? She did bring home a trophy or two from a league she joined.

Having finally read the file folder of papers, I called Stanford and spoke to one of her professors who remembered her well. "She was the most brilliant student I have ever had in my twenty years of teaching graduate courses," he told me.

My mother changed in my eyes. She was no longer simply a bad mother, whose home I escaped at seventeen and returned to only to help her die. She was now a pioneer during an era when women were not allowed to be visionaries. I understood why my mother was crippled with depression. I saw her courage and how diligently she had worked to endow me with her spirit of heart.

With Steve Kent, a director from Los Angeles, and Lauren Elder, a visual artist from Oakland, I developed a performance work about my mother's life and her death. We told the story from multiple points of view: the way I perceived my mother when I was a child; the way my mother experienced me, her daughter, as I was growing up; the way the world perceived my crazy, visionary mother; and my experience as an adult, looking back at my mother's life. Truth could be told only through the lens of multiple vantage points.

Every night after the performance, a few stray women would be waiting in the lobby to talk to me. One by one, they took me aside and confessed that they, too, had been raised by brilliant mothers who, unable to endure the ruling paradigm of the fifties that relegated women to the role of apron-clad, whisk-wielding housewives with perfect manicures, had gone mad one way or another. With tears in their eyes, they thanked me for redeeming their mothers in their eyes. I had not realized until then how common my experience was, nor had they. We were grateful to find one another.

But the biggest reward for me was the movement within my own heart. I had not missed my mother's funeral, but I had missed knowing my mother. As I worked on the piece, I came to understand what my mother had lived through. Forgiveness arose in my heart like one of those big waves surfers go around the world hunting down, a long curve of a wave that happens because of some mysterious action of the earth and the moon, and all you have to do is catch it and ride the curl into shore.

The Practice

After a session of writing down what bugs you, write the same story from the point of view of whoever the perceived enemy is. Go as deeply as you can into the reality of the "other." Look at yourself from the point of view of the other. Look at the world from the vantage point of the other. Feel the other. Be fearless. Write.

You can use "he" or "she" or "I" when you write from the point of view of someone other than yourself. Experiment and find what feels most comfortable and allows you to delve the deepest. You can also use "he" or "she" when you write about yourself, which can give you some distance from a story that feels too personal or confusing to reveal.

Art insists that we tell the whole truth, not simply our blind, accusing, and self-pitying version of it. That is why we are drawn to art, and that is why art is difficult to get right. That is why we hate our art, and that is why we love it. That is why we come back, over and over again, to the feet of the taskmaster, the feet of Art, and offer our paintings and dances and jottings and songs. And that is why sometimes we are humble, sometimes grateful, and sometimes we wish Hannibal Lector would show up and chop off Art's limbs and eat them roasted. And sometimes, teary-eyed with gratitude, we lay flowers at Art's feet. She is a fearless, driving, precise guru who does not let up for an instant and gives no slack as she demands the truth, the whole truth and nothing but, until we roll over and surrender it up.

six

Tea for Two

Creating in Pairs

"Improvisation, composition, writing, painting, theater, invention, all creative acts are forms of play, the starting place of creativity in the human growth cycle, and one of the great primal life functions."

—STEPHEN NACHMANOVITCH

Friend Food

The first few chapters of this book have focused on solitary practices that address our need as individuals to revitalize our lives with creative self-expression. But activities we do in isolation are not sufficient to satisfy our longings—we also have a heartfelt and legitimate craving for deep and funny human contact. Whether or not we are aware of this hunger, it persists within us until we offer our hearts the nourishment of genuine companionship.

Many of us feel alone because, as participants in modern life, we collectively have closed off many of the avenues to intimacy. Yet however alone we may feel, we are not alone in this life. We are surrounded by living beings with whom we are inextricably connected.

The desire for lively and intimate companionship is a healthy human need that is satisfied by simply being who we are, fully and with generosity, in the company of our friends. In the same way that each of us is unique, each friendship has a distinctive personality—a flavor, a taste, a style of being. What we love about our friendships is not only the people who are our friends, but also the ways of being that each friendship gives birth to.

In the same way that we long for freedom as individuals, we also long to feel free in the company of one another. We uncover a path to freedom when we introduce pastimes into our friendships that stimulate what is natural to human behavior: spontaneous and creative acts of self-expression.

Meditation

It just takes a minute. Sit down with your friend, close your eyes, and breathe. That's all. One of you has to be brave enough to suggest it: "Let's meditate for a minute." The other has to be open enough to agree even if they're not exactly in the mood because they've got a lot on their plate and time is ticking away inside their head like a heartbeat on amphetamines: "Good idea."

A colleague I've been working with came rushing through the studio door late for a meeting. The afternoon was hot and sweat was beading on both of our foreheads and the dog lay limp in a shaded corner. We were both talking quickly, interrupting each other because waiting until someone finished a complete sentence was too time consuming, and we had way too much ground to cover in the time allotted. As we pulled our chairs together and reached for our pens and yellow pads, there was a moment's pause and it occurred to me we might meditate for a minute. "Want to meditate?" I asked. My colleague's face lit up as if I had offered her an all-expenses-paid trip to Hawaii. We instantly went silent.

You know that feeling right before you fall asleep for an afternoon nap when you're on vacation and the breeze is coming through an open window and you start to drift off and you wonder why you ever gave up naps, which now seem to be the most pleasant of all human experiences? That's the way I felt. After a couple of minutes, we opened our eyes and we were calm. Then we officially started our meeting and no longer found ourselves trampling on each other's words.

When we take refuge in silence for even a fleeting moment, we shed layers of stress, we see more clearly, and no matter how difficult our lives are, we find a place to rest. Meditation is a time for the noisy intellect and the enterprising opposable thumb to sit back and listen to the whispering heart. Meditation is generally a silent practice—the myriad thoughts bustling in and out of the mind like shoppers through the rotating doors of a department store, shared with no one. So we often conceive of it as a purely private experience. But in fact, when done with others, contemplative practices are deeply bonding and can have profound effects on the quality of our relationships.

We communicate with one another primarily through nonverbal means and much of what we exchange with another person has little to do with words. Sometimes we are graced with a state of mutuality with a friend and communication flows with little effort. At other times we find ourselves at odds and no matter how well we articulate our thoughts and feelings, we do not get through to each other. Through the simple act of being quiet together, we can completely alter the nature of our relating.

———————

As we become quiet, we open to the part of our being that is calm and alert and kind. Or perhaps we are angry or hurt or exhausted and, in becoming aware of our emotional state, can admit it to our friend. Through the act of acknowledgment, we are less likely to cause harm and more likely to take sustenance in our friendships.

When we meditate with a friend, we divest ourselves for a moment of our busyness and together, we touch the silence that resides at the core of all mental, physical, and emotional activity. The silence that lives at the center of our own heart is the same silence that lives within the heart of our companion and as we touch that silence, we are communing.

We need not take an hour or even twenty minutes—we can meditate for a minute or two or three. We need not sit in lotus with our legs crossed. We can sit on a chair or a couch or lie down. And we need not do complex practices—we can simply be quiet together, allowing the mind to settle and the heart to breathe.

We know this, but we forget. We forget because we are hypnotized by talking and doing and thinking, imagining that well-being is found in words and actions and ideas. Upon occasion, however, we get lucky and we listen to the voice that is nudging us to be quiet, not only alone, but with our friends—to take a minute or two to sit and close our eyes and enter the realm of silence.

Meditation is simple. It is we who are complex. But we also are wise and courageous, each and every one of us. No matter how many times we forget, or for how many years, stillness awaits us with great patience. And whenever we remember, stillness is there, at the core of our being, bearing great gifts.

The Practice

When you are with a friend, take a minute, close your eyes, and feel the sensations of breath coming and going. Exert no effort to breathe and instead allow the breath to move in its own rhythm. As attention settles on breath, the breath tends automatically to deepen in the body. Open the belly to breathe.

As you breathe in, invite the mind, the heart, and the body to become calm. As you breathe out, invite all the tension you are holding, consciously and unconsciously, to fall away.

With your companion, settle into the invitation offered by silence to come to rest. When you open your eyes, you will see each other and be glad.

Massage

When she was eleven, my neighbor Annie came to visit after school and mentioned that her back was hurting. She had been in a minor car accident a few days earlier and was still suffering from the impact of the collision. I was frantically busy trying to meet a deadline on an article I was writing. Dirty dishes overflowed from the sink onto the counter. Dust was thick enough on the surfaces of the furniture to invite finger paintings. I had a list of phone calls to make. But I drew a bubble bath for Annie and when she emerged from the tub, I invited her to lie down on my bed and I massaged her back. Her breath deepened and her muscles softened under my touch, and as Annie became calm, so did I. Glancing around my house I no longer felt beleaguered by the blight of chaos but instead noticed the vase of fresh lilies I had set on the bureau that morning and the way the deep red of the tribal rug glowed in the sunlight coming through the sliding glass door.

One of the benefits of giving a massage is that the giver is affected by the quieting that takes place in the receiver—this is the alchemy of touch.

Our friendships thrive on massage. We need not give full body massages or spend oodles of time—we can massage the head, or the feet, or the shoulders for a minute, or two, or three.

But I don't feel like giving anyone a massage because my own back and neck hurt, you say to yourself as your friend reaches his hand to his shoulder and winces. You know he is in pain and that you could take a minute and rub his shoulder and he would feel better. Instead, you move your own hand to your own neck and you, too, wince in pain and together you and your friend complain about this ache and that ache like old folks sitting on the front porch of a beach hotel in Florida, the pink paint peeling from the walls.

We imagine since we are busy and suffering ourselves that we will be further compromised if we offer to care for our friend. While that logic appears to be sound, it is nevertheless wrong; in fact, we will feel better.

You can offer a friend a hand massage when you are having a cup of tea and she is telling you about the man with the code name of Cadet, who seemed utterly attractive on the computer screen, but turned out to only want to talk about his toy soldier collection. Or you can offer a head massage to your friend who is a bit nervous because his teenage daughter, having passed her driving test in the afternoon, insisted on borrowing his car for the evening and is out for the first time alone behind the wheel, cavorting with her friends.

Often we are too shy to offer the gift of our touch and instead offer to mix a double martini. But when we do have the courage, and the wisdom, to assess when the offer is appropriate, we might discover that our friends are deeply grateful to receive even a one-minute massage, and that we enjoy touching as much as our friends enjoy being the recipients of our care.

The Practice

For a week, take on the practice of offering touch to your friends, children, spouse, colleagues.

When you begin a massage, take a moment to let your hands rest on your partner's body without moving. Feel the warmth of the skin, the aliveness of the breathing body under your hands. Then, allow the fingers to find their way. Hands have their own intelligence and can feel the hard hold of muscles that refuse to give, the sensitive places that need light touch—and they know what to do. An aspect of what feels good when we are touched is the quality of the masseur's attention.

If after a week you find that you enjoy the practice, take it on for a month, or a year—or a lifetime.

Partner Dancing

I was standing at the sink doing the dishes on a Saturday morning. My friend, who was visiting from England, was shaving his head in the bathroom. He strode into the kitchen shirtless, his head shining, his pajama pants loose around his thin frame, and he slipped a CD into the player—some deejay mix he had carried with him from London. As he started dancing, I kept washing the dishes, only now I was grumbling to myself about how the oatmeal had stuck to the bottom of the pot and wondering if my friend had made his bed or left it mussed. He sauntered over to me, grabbed my soapy hand, rolled his hips, and looked me straight in the eyes. I couldn't refuse. We danced around the kitchen table and he picked up a dish towel and waved it about like a belly dancer's silk scarf. A few minutes later, we both sashayed over to the sink and while I washed (hips still rocking), my friend dried (in between flurries of kitchen-towel scarf dancing). As we put away the pots and pans, we spun around each other's bodies, cookware in hand, like chefs in a Broadway musical.

Dancing with a friend is good medicine—healing to the body and healthy for the friendship. In some cases, when you've spent many years hanging out with a companion and dancing has not been an activity you've shared, you might encounter difficulty at first—your bodies unsure of how to relate to each other. Here are a couple of movement recipes that might help get you going.

The Practice

When you are hanging out with a friend, spouse, child, lover, or colleague, put on music and dance together. You might be cooking dinner, gardening, watching television, house cleaning, or having a meeting. Take a break and dance.

At some point, dance entirely on your own, moving in a way that is solely dictated by your own body's response to the music. At other points, join your partner and dance together, doing the same movements that your partner is doing. Move back and forth freely between these two options—dancing alone and then dancing together.

When you dance alone, fully commit to the movements you are doing. When one partner dances with intensity, the other partner feels the energy and can be moved into a similar space of energetic clarity. Commitment does not mean that you move fast and big; you can be committed to slow, lyrical movement as well. When you join your partner to move together, maintain your commitment to whatever movements you are executing.

As the dance develops, you might want to occasionally make physical contact, connecting your hands or bumping your hips or moving into traditional couple's dance positions. Then move away again, so that you can find your own private relationship to movement in the company of your friend.

Any place can be transformed into a dance hall: the living room, the kitchen, the bathroom, the bedroom, the elevator, the hallway, the stairwell, the garden.

Mirroring

A few months ago, Corey and I were encountering a great deal of mutual resistance in creating scenes together and found ourselves moving in opposite directions both physically and imaginatively. When Corey was envisaging a scene about an ill father and his promiscuous daughter, I was imagining a scene about a pair of feral dogs. When Corey visualized we were a couple of old men rowing in the sea at dawn, I imagined we were a husband and wife having a fight in a restaurant. When he felt it was time to cut back on language and allow movement to lead, I babbled. When I felt it was time to sing, he fell silent. With the pressure of an upcoming performance heightening our impatience, we were beginning to lose faith in one another.

David, our director, suggested we do the mirroring exercise. I balked. Mirroring was an old theater game I'd done in the sixties—wasn't there a more sophisticated exercise we could do, something more contemporary? David insisted. Reluctantly, I faced Corey, looked into his eyes, and we took turns following each other's movement.

"Slow down, notice facial expressions," David advised, and I adjusted the muscles of my lips and brow to match Corey's. "Move together without either of you leading," David coached, and Corey and I allowed actions to arise as if by themselves, maintaining as perfect a unison as we could manage.

As we continued the work, I felt myself dissolve into Corey as he dissolved into me and the movements emerged as if from a shared body that had a will and direction of its own. The sensation of mutuality was a great relief, but I was not unhappy when David directed us to find an ending and I resided in my body again as its sole occupant, free to fling an arm or collapse to the floor alone. But Corey had not completely retracted from my inner world nor I from his; when we returned to full-out improvising, we found our way into mutual territory with remarkable ease, both of us squarely inside the same story: a couple making plans for a tropical vacation.

We have heard over and over again, from spiritual teachers, that we are not separate but inextricably connected, and this insight has now been confirmed by hard science. Yet we have been conditioned to overlook this fact. Intimacy is scary and Americans, in particular, raised on competition and individualism, prefer maintaining a comfortable degree of discrete singularity to the feeling of identity dissolution. As a result, we are unfamiliar with the strategies of ego-softening that are a prerequisite for effective partnering. The impact of moving in precise simultaneity with another can be surprisingly profound. When we follow our partner's lead, we feel as though we are merging with our partner; and when we take the lead and see ourselves reflected back in our partner's moves, that revelation, too, can be startling in its intimacy.

Any way we go about it, by divesting ourselves of the feeling of separation, we also divest ourselves of the psychological barriers to creative collaboration, and our partnerships take on new dimensions that further our work and our pleasure.

While teaching a course in communication and team building to the employees of a software company, I invited the participants to do mirroring. For many of them, this was the first time since compulsory ballroom dance classes in junior high school that they found themselves engaged in a partnering exercise involving movement. But they gallantly forged ahead. Nevertheless, I could see the hesitation in the way they worked, the movements stiff and premeditated. As the practice unfolded and the pleasure of spontaneous play became apparent, their reluctance subsided. Tension fell away from faces, bodies moved with ease, and the room became alive with energy.

Weeks later, I asked the participants if they had noticed any changes in their working environment. They reported that they felt considerably more relaxed with one another, the ease apparent not only in coffee room banter, but also in interactions around the meeting table. Creativity tends to flourish in a relaxed environment—and this is true if we are talking about the interior of a person's mind, or the feeling of a partnership, or the ambience of a group. Most of us could benefit from having a director in our living room or our workplace saying, "Okay everyone, the atmosphere around here is way tense, now take a minute and do mirroring." A director who would force us to obey.

Mirroring, massage, movement, and meditation enhance what in the theater world is called "tuning." When the tuning between actors is sharp and subtle, the acting takes on an authenticity and clarity, the players moving in and out of scenes together with a noticeable harmony of language and gesture. The benefits of tuning can be of use to all of us in both our personal and our professional lives. When we feel in sync with a partner or friend, whatever activity we engage in takes on a quality of flow.

To create harmony in our partnerships, we can engage in practices that acknowledge the vast realm of nonverbal ground in which our relationships reside. We can learn to feel one another and respond with feeling, rather than attempting to live in our minds. We can soften our notions of separation and strengthen our felt experience of connection.

The Practice

Face your partner as if looking into a mirror. Decide who will be the first to lead. Look into each other's eyes. Partner A begins moving slowly, making sure the movements are so easy that Partner B can follow without difficulty. Perhaps she begins by slowly lifting her arms until they reach shoulder level and then lowering them again. Then she might lift them again, but this time continue until her arms are extended above her head. Partner B executes the movements as precisely as possible, maintaining unison with his partner. After half a minute or whatever "feels right," Partner A says, "Switch," and Partner B takes over the leadership. B might lift a leg, or take a long slow step sideways. A follows, keeping as precise a unison as possible. After thirty seconds or so, B says, "Switch," and A takes over the leadership. And so on, back and forth.

After a few minutes have passed and each partner has had several turns at leading, try dropping leadership altogether and allow the movement to arise by itself. Move slowly enough that you can maintain unison. You will find yourselves working together as if by magic—bending forward as you look into each other's eyes, walking sideways in slow motion.

Don't worry if you cannot sustain unbroken leaderless unison. At some point one or the other of you might lead for a moment before leaderless unison is reestablished. No problem. That is the nature of this work. You also might find yourself thinking that your partner is leading while your partner is convinced that you are leading. One of the benefits of the exercise is that you lose the sense of where the movement impulse is coming from as the boundaries between you begin to dissolve.

Remember that the intention of this exercise is to move in unison. To do this well, it is important to keep the movements easy to follow—turning a hand slowly from palm upturned to palm downturned; tilting sideways from the waist and then rising again.

As you become fluent at this game, you will develop the capacity to move more quickly and introduce more complex gestures. This is very exciting as the sense of leadership completely falls away.

Okay, you've read the exercise, you understand it, and you're even somewhat interested in doing it. But you don't do it. You can't find the time to take five minutes out of a business meeting with your partner to do something as weird as moving around the office in unison. And you certainly don't have the time at home with the phone ringing and dinner to get on the table and your kid needing a bath. Not that you think it's a stupid exercise; you get the point, but it isn't an essential need and you only have time right now for the essentials.

Frankly, I understand your position, and mirroring won't make your life less busy. Unfortunately, reading the exercise is not sufficient if you want to derive the benefit. To benefit, you have to do it. If you don't have five minutes, do it for one minute. If you don't have one minute, take thirty seconds. Your mood might lift, your partnership might amuse you. And then you will continue with your business meeting, with preparing dinner, with bathing your kid, but you might have more fun.

One Sentence at a Time

When I was a girl growing up in Los Altos, I spent many afternoons curled up with my best friend, Nancy, over the fat-as-a-Bible Sears catalog. We chose wedding gowns and fiancés and living room sets and chaise lounges as we fantasized a future in ranch-style houses with clipped lawns. Despite all the New Age formulas about reality unfolding the way you want it to if you visualize with precision and conviction, I did not end up in a house on a cul-de-sac with a patio where a pink umbrella shaded potato chips and onion dip while a husband in Bermudas barbecued with a shiny spatula in his pot-mitted hand. But I did have a blast making up stories with Nancy.

Imagining characters with lives of their own is a pleasure for the psyche. And while creating stories in solitude has many rewards, creating a narrative with a companion allows you a shared and private reality the way building a fort in the backyard did when you were a kid.

But there is more to collaborative creation than the pleasure of a brief fling of mutual imagination. As we join forces with a companion to create an alternate reality, we actually give voice to issues harbored in the subconscious. Our characters live out our inner conflicts, reveal our secrets, enact what we are unable to express and so provide the psyche with a measure of healing.

We can all benefit from giving our psyches a metaphorical campfire around which to tell stories. One evening, instead of going to the video store and renting a story in a box, turn down the lights, lay back, and start: "Once upon a time . . ."

The Practice

Sit down with a friend. Get comfortable. Taking turns, build a story one sentence at a time.

For example:

X begins: "Five more weeks of work," Geraldine thought.

Y continues: The phone had been ringing all day.

X: She had left people on hold for minutes listening to Muzak and company advertisements.

Y: So by the time she actually talked to them, they were angry and irritated and mean.

X: "Five more weeks of work before I can go on vacation," she thought.

Y: Salmon fishing in Alaska.

X: Last year, she had been the only woman on an eighteen-person trip.

Y: There, she had seen the black bear.

X: That's what everyone called him.

Y: He drove an eighteen-wheeler and smelled of cheap cologne.

X: He made the trip from Missoula to Anchorage three times a month.

Y: And told her witty tales about his family.

X: She liked the way his eyes twinkled and was never one to care if a man had a family.

Y: "Five more weeks of work," she said as the phone rang again.

X: "Then I'll be heading for Alaska."

Begin by keeping the stories brief. If you have some time to play, make up a few stories. Then experiment with longer ones.

X says: Paul looked in the three-way mirror and realized the pants he was trying on were too short.

Y continues: He needed a suit for his bar mitzvah which was only two days away, but he refused to buy one that didn't fit him perfectly even though his mother was claiming this one was fine, just fine.

Remember, don't get attached to how you think the story *should* develop. Follow your companion's input, allowing the partnership to have its own creative life independent of your personal wishes for the direction the story could take. You might be thinking that Paul will end up with an elegant Armani just in time to step up to the *bimah*, while your partner is imagining that the tasteless mother prevails, and as Paul chants the haftorah, all he can think about is the inch of bare skin between his sock and the cuff of his pants. And then what happens as the story unfolds is that the rabbi's wife choked on a fishbone during Sabbath dinner, and as the rabbi successfully performed the Heimlich maneuver he threw his back out and had to be hospitalized, and the bar mitzvah was postponed. What makes collaboration so delightful is the element of surprise. Let go of preconceptions as you work, and allow the story to unfold with your full participation but free of your control.

The Eros of Song

When I was in my early twenties, I took a course on shamanism at Esalen Institute. Toward the end of the workshop, we were to venture out into the woods with a sleeping bag and a jug of water and spend the night alone. I had befriended a tall and lanky young man with wavy hair and horn-rimmed glasses who wrote science fiction stories. We set out together on a path along a creek through a forest of towering redwoods, intending to part at some point and go our separate ways. A couple of miles into the woods, however, we discovered a cave carved out by fire in the trunk of an ancient tree, and we both unfurled our sleeping bags and settled in. Night fell with a blanket of darkness. We nestled two candles into the dirt floor and began to sing. We did not sing songs we knew, but made up melodies on the spot that emerged from whatever we were feeling at the moment. Our voices wove in and out of each other, found harmonies, and entered extended moments of unison. We were not physically touching and yet I felt an extraordinary commingling.

Bodies are thick and weighty but the voice, made of air, can diffuse into a partner's voice until it no longer feels separate from the other because it has blended fully like sugar melting in warm water. Vocal duets can feel like lovemaking as voices touch and permeate each other. We sense this musical intimacy when two vocalists sing well together. We hear their separate voices, but we also hear the blend of sound that they make—and the merged sound is what moves us, the two becoming one.

Many of us feel a lack of exuberance and playfulness in our relationships with partners, friends, and children, our style of relating dulled by the habits of our day-to-day lives. Singing together can alleviate this felt sense of monotony. We do not need to know the lyrics of songs to sing together. We can make up sounds and melodies, any time, any place.

The Practice

When you are with a friend, take a break from whatever you are doing and sing a song you both know. A familiar song like "Row, Row, Row Your Boat" or "This Little Light of Mine" or "A Bicycle Built for Two": one that is very easy to sing.

Sing the song a few times together, and then drop the words and carry on singing the melody with na-na-na, or la-la-la, or do-be-do. When you feel at ease and solid with the melody, improvise together. You might add a harmony line, or a bass line, or a rhythmic riff, or just slip in a few extra notes here and there, grace notes.

If this is easy for you, try improvising a melody from scratch. One person begins with a simple phrase of melody, taking perhaps eight beats and using a single syllable such as na-na-na or la-la-la or do-do-do. Then repeat this simple phrase over and over again. The partner joins and sings along, in unison.

When the basic melody line is clearly established, begin to improvise by adding a drone, a harmony part, or a percussive part. Sing without effort, without thinking, with great ease, allowing the composition to develop in whichever direction the melody chooses to unfold. Continue until you find an organic finish together.

After one round, repeat the practice with the other partner introducing the beginning phrase. And remember, keep it simple.

While some people take quite easily to singing together, others experience difficulty. Either way, stick with the practice for a while and iron out the glitches. After a brief time of practicing, you will make progress and find that you can actually sing well together.

Remember not to attempt to impress one another with your inspired creativity or virtuosity. Instead, devote yourselves to listening and supporting what is emerging. Adjust your voice to suit the voice of your partner so that you are blending your sounds.

Whether singing is easy for someone or challenging, the only way to become fully at home in the realm of song is to practice singing. As we practice, we make remarkable progress and the payoff is worth whatever initial effort or discomfort we might experience.

Each partnership has its own strengths and weaknesses. I have had the experience of doing a sound duet with a complete stranger that was seamlessly harmonious, and doing a sound duet with an improvising partner that was jagged and confusing despite our many years of working together. Each time we engage in the improvisation, the work will be different. Rather than hoping to be perfectly accomplished at it, we can aim at being perfectly experimental, open to whatever happens, open to refining our relationships to one another through the medium of sound, and slowly developing our skills of play and our skills of relationship.

Talk to a Stranger

Sometimes we are lonely not because we do not have a kind and devoted partner, or a bevy of good friends who make us laugh, or a family to spend holidays eating turkey with, but for no reason we can name. We roam about on errands feeling as if we are shrouded in a protective coating that separates us from the mass of humankind with whom we are sharing subway cars, offices, public parks, gyms, movie theaters. We imagine we are safe inside our cocoon, when we are actually suffering from a vague malaise.

One of the pleasures of traveling is meeting people on the road who are generally outside the scope of our normal milieu. On a train in France I met a man who specialized in Russian sacred choral music, and as we rolled along the Côte d'Azur, he placed his headphones over my ears and I was drenched in heavenly, freshly recorded harmonies. In Paris, I met a journalist who was an expert in Soviet espionage, and he told me the stories of famous spies as we drank lemonade at an outdoor café.

While it seems easier to engage strangers in conversation when I'm far away from home, I've learned that I can have similar moments of connection in my own neck of the woods. People's lives are fascinating and an entire novel can be inspired by the seed of a spontaneous conversation with a stranger. Suddenly the invisible coating that separates us falls away and we find ourselves connected.

A Tibetan lama was giving teachings at Esalen one morning and told of how when he first visited the United States he felt as though he were in a god realm—lights ablaze, the food abundant and fresh, the cars shiny and purring, the clothes clean and colorful, whatever one wished for within reach. A companion drove him across the Golden Gate Bridge and the lama was dazzled by the views of the bay dappled with sailboats and islands and the alabaster city catching the glow of the setting sun.

"The bridge is very famous because people jump off of it to commit suicide," his guide explained.

The lama was stupefied. How, under this glorious arch with these heavenly views in this realm of abundance does anyone feel the urge to end a precious human life? But after a few weeks in the United States, the lama began to understand such despair.

He told us how in Tibet when a villager walking along a mountain path encountered a stranger walking toward him, they would both stop to talk. Their conversations were very personal—about their spousal relationships, the politics of the village, their children. And then, after an hour, or two, the travelers would continue on their way. What was important in life was not time, but the quality of human relationship.

Many years ago, a screenwriter friend of mine was commissioned to develop a script about the destruction of the Amazon. During his many weeks of research there, he met a shaman named Davi Kopenawa Yanomami. "When the white man came, the first thing he gave us was his diseases," the shaman explained. "The Yanomami have cures for their sickness; they are part of the agreement between the people and the forest. But the Yanomami have no cure for your diseases. I have seen the white man's civilization . . . his cities, his unhappiness. Everyone here is dying of your sadness and your diseases and the disease of your heart."

If we are to heal from the disease of loneliness that modern life imparts, we are the ones who must find the remedy.

The Practice

In the grocery store or at the movie theater, on a bus or a subway, at a café or in a bookstore, at the airport, or the gym, find someone you don't know and strike up a conversation. Be friendly. Ask questions. Show interest. Show care.

You can take on this practice as a performance piece for a week or two. Each day, talk to a stranger, and each day, document the encounter with a photograph or a journal entry or a sketch or a short short story. Our experience of life is transformed when we connect with one another.

We can only end the epidemic of isolation if we make contact. We cannot wait for our culture to change by some act of universal grace. It is we who are the instruments of grace, we who through our words and our actions acknowledge that we are not alone on this earth, but together.

". . . it may take you many years to find out that the stranger you talked to once for half an hour in the railroad station may have done more to point you to where your true homeland lies than your priest or your best friend or even your psychiatrist."

—FREDERICK BUECHNER

Art Sparring

My friend, Bharath, having been educated at Oxford, uses language in a way that is uncommon to Americans: his sentences are long, well-crafted, infused with a dry wit, and laced with multisyllabic words. I find that when I talk with him my own sentences become more exalted, and I revel in our extended conversations. One night, however, we launched into a heated and not at all pleasant discussion. After an hour, he interrupted me midsentence and said, "That metaphor you used was completely incorrect." Without a moment's pause, I retorted, "Well you've been spewing run-on sentences full of shifting verb tenses." We looked at each other with bitter gazes, and then laughed. We returned to our fight, but our feelings toward one another had softened and we could no longer take our positions so seriously.

When embroiled in a difficult discussion with a friend or colleague, we can become so polarized around a particular issue that we lose track of who the other person is and what they mean to us. We see them only in the light of the current crisis. We might know from our spiritual practice, or our sessions with psychotherapists, that when we are caught in a knot of hurt our point of view is skewed by our tendency to project old wounds onto current dilemmas, and so perceive reality through the lens of our own conditioning. And yet we find that even when we know our vision is muddied by delusion, we still hold fast to our positions.

When wounded, we tend to enter a trance that can only perceive perpetrator and victim, and until this trance is lifted, understanding cannot emerge. It is important to learn to protect ourselves from emotional and physical harm, and to negotiate with our partners to have our needs met. But we can also learn skills that lessen the pain of psychological knots by injecting an element of play into our relationships at the very moment of greatest difficulty.

The only way conflicts can be resolved is from the wisdom of an empathic heart. Play, by inviting the heart to fully express itself, also opens the heart to understand the state of the other—the loved one or cherished friend or work colleague who has become a sudden enemy. While play may not be the ultimate resolution to the conflicts that arise, it can be a method to alleviate the grip of our frozen points of view so that understanding can emerge, and out of this understanding agreements can be reached to ease our suffering.

One of the core teachings offered by Thich Nhat Hanh is that compassion arises out of understanding. The formula for the resolution of human conflict has nothing to do with proving that our own point of view is objectively true, that our individual needs are somehow more important and ethical and substantial than the needs of the other, but instead has to do with understanding that all points of view are subjective. When we transform our well-founded grievances into art, we loosen the bonds of self-referencing and begin to broaden our sight lines.

The Practice

PAINT SPAR

The next time you find yourself in a fight with a spouse, lover, friend, parent, sibling, or child, pull out your art supplies. Post the paper on the wall if you have a studio or playroom, or roll it out across the dining table or the floor. As you fight, mark the paper with paint. Instead of each person making separate drawings, mark on each other's marks. Throw paint at the paper, slap paint on the paper, use your fingers like you did in kindergarten.

If you prefer not to deal with the mess of paint, use colored pens or pencils, chalk or pastels. If you don't have a roll of paper, cover the wall or the table or the floor with newspaper and paint on that; go out on the driveway and paint the cement.

Work as physically as possible, moving the whole body, allowing each mark to be a bodily expression of whatever feelings are arising at the moment.

Make furious marks. Make hurt marks. Make huge marks with great vigor. Or tiny, scratchy marks in a corner. If you fill up one piece of paper, unfurl another.

If you cannot bring yourself to art spar with the person with whom you are fighting, do the practice with a friend. Get together, roll out the paper, and make art.

seven

When Gathered

Group Play

"The actor is able to approach in himself a cosmic dread as large as his life. He is able to go from this dread to a joy so sweet that it is without limit."

—JOSEPH CHAIKIN

Sangha

In many ways, the discussion of creativity in community is the heart of this book. We can experience great personal freedom of expression and learn to frolic in partnership with abandon, but without a community of friends with whom we can work as an ensemble, we will still live in a fractured world. Thich Nhat Hanh has said that in every era a Buddha arises—a person of great spiritual wisdom whose radiance touches millions of people. The next Buddha to manifest, he predicts, will not be an individual, but will be the sangha, the diverse community of people who in their dedication to awakening the heart and mind will have a profound effect on the unfolding of human history. *We will be the Buddha* if, as a community, we have the courage to devote our lives to the unfolding of wisdom and compassion.

We do not live independently of one another but are deeply intertwined. Like the proverbial butterfly deep in the Amazon, who by flapping his wings affects the weather patterns halfway around the globe, everything we do sends out waves of effects in a seamless pattern of interbeing. Many of us long to bring the awareness of interconnectedness to the foreground of our experience, to celebrate and give expression to the web of relations.

We can sing alone, but can only achieve harmony if we sing in a chorus. We can dance alone, but can only experience the joy of tribal energy when we dance together. We can pray and meditate alone, but when we pray and meditate together we are lifted up and sustained by the collective. With a commitment to the bonding that self-expression engenders, we can emerge from our seclusion and, in so doing, address not only our individual needs but also the wounds of the world.

I offer two types of group practices—one in which everyone works together at the same time, and another in which an individual or duet works while others observe. While most of us experience mortal terror at the thought of performing, we also (even though we are loath to admit it) hunger to be witnessed. The audience provides energy for the performer who, feeding on the light of attention, can reach levels of clarity and prowess that are not available without the presence of the observer. We enjoy performing not only because we crave love and mistakenly hope the audience can provide what our families often fail to—pure and unadulterated adulation—but also because we revel in the heightened state of being that calls forth our wittiest, wisest, and most authentic self.

In my workshops, after a round of solo or duet performances, the room takes on a soft glow of mutual appreciation. We come to know one another in a way that ordinary conversation does not accomplish, and we experience bonds of affection that extend beyond the walls of the room and into the fabric of one another's lives.

A Round of Singing

In 1990, I was invited to visit the Soviet Union to participate in a tour of the Volga with artists and peace activists from around the world. Peristroika was unfolding, and the country was on the brink of vast changes, celebrating a momentous period of dawning social freedom. Every few days we would dock at a different port and mount a spectacle of performances in grand multitiered theaters to audiences who tossed bouquets and stomped their feet and thundered with applause.

Toward the end of the tour, the anthropologist friend with whom I was traveling expressed an interest to the Russian organizers in visiting a region where shamanistic practices were still conducted by tribal peoples. A bureaucrat snatched up our passports without explanation and, several days later, a blond guide in a red suit handed us train tickets and swept us off on an itinerary that was not fully disclosed.

After an all-night train ride, we debarked in a northern city near the border of Finland. A group of Russia's master restorers of Gothic churches met us at the station. Rather than heading for Tuva lands to investigate ancient tribal rituals and throat singing, which is where we had intended to travel, we were mysteriously ushered aboard a passenger ferry that flew inches above the water across a grand lake to Kidji Island, the site of a renowned wooden cathedral sprouting a multitude of onion domes.

As night fell, our hosts invited us to Finnish baths in old wooden saunas. The men crowded into one where they sweated and swigged vodka and beat each other's bare skin with the medicinal leaves of willow branches. The women cloistered in a neighboring sauna, slapping backs and thighs and breasts with myrtle leaves. When the heat became unbearable, we plunged into the cold lake just footsteps down a muddy path, and cooled ourselves so that we could reenter the antique hut for another round of steam and branch beating.

Afterward, we gathered in a small cottage with bunk-filled bedrooms and piled into the kitchen. My hosts, who had been young children when the Iron Curtain fell, had never met Americans before. They had only heard about the evil empire across the oceans, where the rich lived in mansions and the poor lived homeless and hungry on sidewalks and the government, intent on over-taking the world, pointed nuclear warheads at Moscow. I, too, had been a child during the Cold War, and when elementary school was interrupted by the undulating screams of an air raid siren, I had dutifully scrambled under my desk, covering my neck with one hand and my eyes with another, prac-ticing for the day when an atomic bomb was launched by the satanic Communists. Decades later, here we were together, Russians and Americans around an old kitchen table, red-cheeked and wet-haired and hungry and deeply relieved. Finding the enemy human, we celebrated with vodka, a jar of peas, tins of sardines, boiled potatoes, a hunk of cheese, and thin slices of dark, sour bread.

In the middle of the meal, one of the men leaned back in his chair and began to sing, his voice thick and deep. With a full beard, long wavy hair, and an angelic face, he resembled an icon on the wall of one of the churches he had so masterfully restored. When he finished, the man sitting beside him crossed his beefy arms over his hefty belly and bellowed out another song. Everyone offered a song: a lullaby, a folk song, a hymn. One man could barely hold a tune, but he belted out a ballad without hesitation. A woman with pale skin and big blue eyes, her hair a frizzy red halo around her head, sang an airy song, quiet and moving. My friend hey-yah-yah-ed a Navajo chant she had learned from a medicine man, and I sang a Hebrew prayer I had learned from my Russian grandma.

The notion that singing was something only for children or professional musicians had not entered the minds of my Russian hosts. The notion that singing was only for people who could hold a tune had also not occurred to them. Singing was for everyone, for men and women and children and these Americans who had come from an enemy world. Singing was for us.

Something happened around that singing table that talk could not have accomplished, something intimate and playful, spirited and yet deeply serious—we fell in love, all of us with everyone. Singing, we no longer saw each other as alien but recognized each other as kin.

The Practice

When you are gathered with your friends or family, after dinner, or at a party, in the car, around a fire or on a picnic—try singing. Invite each person to sing a song, solo, a song that has resonance for the singer.

We all know the lyrics to at least one song. Many of us commonly choose a Beatles song, but perhaps you have a song that resides more deeply in the heart: a hymn from church, a prayer from synagogue, a chant, a lullaby, the first song you ever learned and that you have sung all your life, privately. Or you can make up a melody in the moment.

Don't worry about holding a tune, needing a microphone or

musical accompaniment, or remembering all the words. Simply sing from the heart, fully. You might feel like singing very softly, or bellowing.

Regardless of how well or how poorly we sing, we take delight in witnessing an inner character in each other come forth, the character who sings. Skill has no relevance; it is only important that you sing. With feeling. With gusto. With panache.

Similar to many of the other exercises in this book, to sing in front of people requires courage. But the joy of singing is well worth whatever initial discomfort might arise. Take the risk. We hide because we are afraid that we are incompetent, that we will embarrass ourselves, that we will go unloved. But it is the very hiding that makes us less appealing. When we drop the masks and emerge as ourselves, effortlessly and without pretense, that is when we are radiant, that is when we are free.

Simultaneous Lecture

Most of the time, we go on about this and that, and we really don't know what we're talking about. But in an effort to win the love and admiration of our children, colleagues, and parents (who never managed to love us sufficiently when we were children, but might one day if we somehow manage to prove our expertise at something), we spout fountains of nonsense with a feigned but eager confidence. Simultaneous lecture, a game that entails giving a believable lecture about an obscure topic you know absolutely nothing about, provides some relief because we can reap rewards, not by our expertise, but by our ability to fake it.

The first time I played this game, I experienced serious apprehension that I would be incapable of coming up with a single notion. And then, as I launched into the lecture, I was amazed at how easily theories spewed forth from my mouth and how familiar this felt, carrying on about something as if I knew what I was talking about when actually, I was making everything up. And I saw in an electrifying instant (like a near-death experience when your whole life flashes by in a nanosecond) how I commonly pretend to know more than I do. We are all posturing and feigning because we imagine that our value as humans is based on how much information we have amassed, as if life were a game show, and so we extrapolate on what we do know and make up what we do not know. As I played the game, everyone listening was well aware I knew not a jot about what I was saying, and for once, I was not *supposed* to know any-thing. This is what makes the game so amusing—as we launch into a round of false command, we take pleasure in the permission to be openly, rather than covertly, speaking nonsense.

At the same time that you are giving your lecture, your partner is also giving a lecture. You are both talking at the same time to an audience who is listen-ing to both of you talk at the same time. And in addition to raving about the history and use of the knitting needle in Sardinia during the pre-Raphaelites or the construction of whalebone corsets and the New England postrevolu-tion economy, you are to incorporate a word or phrase here and there in your own lecture that you have heard your partner use. For instance, one partner might say, "Knitting needles in Sardinia were made by carving the heartwood of blue pine into foot-long needles, with a diameter of one centimeter. The needles were then rubbed hard with a black stone to remove the splinters." His partner might say, "Corsets in New England, in addition to utilizing whale bones, also incorporated the hand-carved bark of blue pine that was rubbed with a black stone."

In order to accomplish this task, you have to listen to what your partner is saying. The ability to talk while someone else is talking and at the same time hear what they are saying is a useful skill for improvisers. Audiences are im-pressed when two simultaneous story lines emerge and then magically weave together. But even if we have no intention of ever performing in an improvi-sation ensemble, by practicing incorporation we develop the ability to blend the ideas of a partner with our own and to derail the more common tendency of refusing entry to another's concepts.

Most of us are afraid of speaking in public; the heart flutters, the stomach churns, sweat gushes. But if we can endure such discomfort and proceed, most of us discover we enjoy being the center of attention and giving voice to our take on things. Simultaneous Lecture is a practice that can assist us in de-veloping some ease and comfort in front of an audience. As we gain confi-dence in our ability to extemporize, we participate more freely in group gatherings—professional meetings, dinner parties, public forums. The per-formance anxiety may not entirely subside, but we have the confidence we can be articulate and amusing so we pay less attention to it.

The Practice

Two people volunteer to work. Two other people from the group offer lecture topics. Make sure that the speakers know *absolutely nothing* about the topics on which they will lecture. If they admit to knowing anything at all about the subjects, junk them and come up with others.

Example topics:

The use of calligraphy in Kazakhstan between 1702 and 1706 and how it influenced the trade of mustangs

Ancient Greek chants used in preparation for childbirth compared to the tonalities used in Chinese opera of the fifteenth century

The speakers talk at the same time as each other about the topics they have been assigned and incorporate single words or phrases that they hear each other speaking. For instance, one person might say, "The pen tips used by the Kazakhstanis were made from the beaks of a blue-feathered bird found in the northernmost regions of the country."

His partner might at the same time be saying, "A Greek custom popular in the northernmost regions of the country was one in which the women, dressed in blue feathers, ululated as they stood in a circle around the birthing mother."

The task, in addition to giving a coherent and believable lecture on the assigned topic, is to listen to the other speaker so that, as much as humanly possible, you are tracking your partner's speech at the same time as delivering your own.

Depression Party

My friend Sheilah called and told me she was tohhhtally depressed. "Me, too," I said, happy to have company. The one thing I cannot stomach when I am miserable is for a good friend to call and tell me how fabulously happy she is because everything in her life is going so well—she is having out-of-this-world sex with her husband and has just won a Pulitzer Prize and her parents, whom she adores because they have been sooooo supportive of her career as an artist her entire life, are celebrating her success by buying her a house in Tuscany and she has just lost ten pounds. That, I cannot stand. So I was pleased to hear that Sheilah was in the dumps, and we spent a half hour on the phone complaining about how our relationships were crumbling and our careers were going nowhere and how we had gained five pounds by eating celery and only on *very* rare occasions dropping into the See's on Fourth Street where they give you a free chocolate even if you are just browsing the truffles.

"We have to dooooo something," Sheilah, who is a jazz vocalist, crooned. We thought about going to the ocean but knew since we lived in the Bay Area and it was summer that the beach would be dripping with fog, which would make us even more depressed. A movie? Couldn't bear the thought of sitting in a dark room with people eating popcorn. Finally, we landed on the notion of throwing a party—a depression party.

We told our guests to wear black and we served black food: black caviar, black sesame crackers, black bean dip, black coffee, dark chocolate. We had black plates and black napkins and black candles. And when anyone asked how you were, you had to say you were terrible, horrible, awful, and complain about all the disgusting, demoralizing, deflating, disease-ridden events happening in your life: traffic school, tragic romance, global warming, financial disaster, unending colds, flea infestations, root canals, career dives. After only a few minutes of kvetching, people started to feel much better and when asked how they were, they were desperate to say, "Fine, I'm having a great time," but we wouldn't let them.

Finally, we could not utter one more word of bad news, and giddiness welled up inside us, and we put on loud music, and we danced.

The "Pelican Dance"

Many years ago, I spent several weeks on Isla de la Piedra, a long, skinny island across the bay from Mazatlán with miles of white sand beaches. In the evenings, I watched the sun slip into the sea as brown pelicans flew in a long parade across a pink-and-salmon sky. A leader pelican seemed to be directing the flight pattern while the other great birds followed behind like a Busby Berkeley chorus. As I studied their dips and rises and the way the big-winged birds soared in the curl of cresting waves, I saw, or perhaps "felt" is the better word, that they were operating not as single individuals but as a unified body. Their communication, which was so precise that they could move in perfect unison, did not seem to be occurring purely in response to an individual's sense of wind currents and sighting of prey, but also in response to a mutual and simultaneous sensing of each other's impulses. Witnessing this simultaneity, I felt a rush of pleasure because I recognized in the movement of pelicans what I had always felt to be true: we do not exist as isolated individuals encased in an envelope of skin, but are connected through an invisible web whose nature we do not yet fully understand but nevertheless sense.

Upon returning home to my studio in downtown Oakland, I began to work on a performance based on the many images I had collected while traveling. I invited a group of men friends to experiment with a movement score I called the "Pelican Dance." Basing the movement on the flight patterns of pelicans, we worked with a follow-the-leader structure, exploring unison group movement and chain movement (as one dancer circled his arms, the next would follow, and then the next and by the time the movement had reached the last dancer, the leader would have established a new movement that would travel down the chain).

We rehearsed for weeks. Over time the men became increasingly receptive to each other's subtle impulses, and able to switch leadership seamlessly, moving like a single body. After the final performance of our run, the men, reluctant to disband, named themselves The Pelicans and continued to meet to experience the pleasure of moving and communing.

We appear to be distinct individuals with separate lives, and on one level, we are. But, on another level, we are not as separate as we might imagine. All of us have had experiences that hint at the existence of interconnectivity: the phone rings just as we are thinking of the person who is calling, an aunt pays a dream visit and later we discover that she passed away at the very moment we dreamt of her, we say the exact words a friend utters at precisely the same time.

If we examine our experience deeply, we cannot determine a distinct boundary between one thing and another. My father, a scientist who spent many years in the field of surface chemistry, explained to me one afternoon as we looked out over the San Francisco Bay that there is no definite point where the sky and the water meet; as the sky nears the surface of the ocean, it takes on elements of the water, and as the ocean nears the sky, it takes on elements of the air so there is a continuum rather than a demarcation point between the two bodies.

We are all made of what we consider to be other than ourselves. We breathe molecules of oxygen that were once part of a tree and are now part of us, which we breathe out into the universe again where they become integrated into the body of yet another being. We eat carrot molecules that were once part of the earth and are now a part of us and then pass through us becoming earth again. Our children are made from our own molecules and we are all made from stardust. So who are we?

When I was in India visiting Poonjaji, I paused one day to admire a white cow dozing in the middle of the road. The cow awoke and looked at me with her big brown eyes, and what I saw was not the cow but the light of consciousness shining through her eyes. And I recognized the cow's consciousness as the same consciousness that flowed through my own eyes, allowing me to see the cow. I saw myself looking back at myself, and I saw that this unified consciousness, which we also call love, is the very fabric of all being in the universe. It is infused in each particle of matter, the essential nature and connective tissue of all and everything. Then the cow stood up, took a dump, and wandered down the street as traffic careened around her.

Each of us is an individual, and at the same time we are a vast spaciousness of being that has no boundaries and includes all beings and all time. Most spiritual practices point us to an understanding of this unity—of how we are interwoven with all and everything—and when we touch this experience as a felt reality, even for a fleeting moment, a wave of well-being rushes over us, and we feel not as if something fantastically exotic has happened, but as though we have finally relaxed into the most familiar and mundane aspect of who we have always known ourselves to be. Many of us taste this dissolution of separate self at moments of grace: when we melt into a profound sexual embrace, when we witness an infant being born, when we enter trance through hard dancing, when we sit on a meditation pillow for weeks on end following our breath, when we do ceremonies with sacred plants, when we pray. And some of us have felt it dancing in unison with a group of our friends, flying across the floor like pelicans.

The Practice

You can do this practice in the living room, on the beach, in a dance studio, or a backyard. One person takes the lead and moves across the floor, walking at a good pace. As she moves, the others follow in a line and imitate in precise unison the movements the leader executes. The leader proceeds slowly enough so that everyone can follow with ease, and when she has had her fill of leadership, she moves the group into a circle and a new leader emerges.

You can experiment with unison movement and also with sequential movement: the leader lifts his arm, then the next dancer lifts his arm, then the next, until the movement has traveled down the line.

Work in silence at the beginning, and then if you like, play music and move. Experiment with many kinds of music so that the vocabulary of the dance is enriched.

If you continue to work with the same group over time, you will refine your tuning and develop subtlety of communication, and the dancing can become more complex. But you do not need a steady group to do this practice; you can do it anytime, anywhere, with anyone.

As we watch a pod of dolphins leaping together, or a litter of puppies wrestling, or seals swimming around each other's sleek bodies, we witness the pleasure of group play and feel a resonance in our own bodies. This impulse to play together is a part of who we are, and some argue, essential to our well-being.

Sound Circle

Singing in a group, creating harmonies and soundscapes and rhythmic relationships, effects that the single voice, no matter how skilled at overtone chanting or scat singing or hymn rendering cannot alone achieve, is one of the great pleasures available to us as humans. And we are not alone in our impulse to form chorales: animals sing together, unleashing their tweets and twitter-ings, honks and howls, barks and bays in forests and meadows and marshes in an ardent announcement of mating season or danger or dawn. For eons, we beings have "joined our voices in song," our voices blending in the creation of a composite sound that is singular yet made of a multiplicity. We who live in such isolation from one another, we who hunger for community, find a mo-ment of relief in the moment of song.

Because most of us no longer sing together when we gather for social events, we can experience difficulty establishing the inroads to song. Impeded by our fear of inadequacy, we repress our voices in a way no bird or dog or wolf or whale or chimpanzee would without threatening its very survival. Our survival might also be threatened by our repression of song, but unaware of the mysterious link between well-being, song, and community, we imagine we can give up song without a price. How odd that we have turned away so vehemently from the activities that give rise to contentment and argue with conviction that we cannot sing and so do not sing. In truth, every single human being is born with the capacity to sing, just as robins, terns, dolphins, and wolves are born with the capacity to loose their voices and carol in commu-nity.

"Sound Circle" is a score for ensemble vocal improvisation built on sound phrases. The composition is constructed and deconstructed one element at a time, the coming together and taking apart of the elements lending the score its dynamic movement. The fundamental guideline is that each participant is to add a sound phrase to the mix that fits in some way with what has already been constructed.

The Practice

Sit in a circle. One person begins with a short sound phrase that has a
clear rhythm and can be easily repeated, over and over again. The
phrase can be a short, eight-beat melody, or a rhythmic phrase (bum
da da bum, bum da da bum). Everyone lightly taps out the established
rhythm.

As the first singer continues his phrase, the person next to him
joins in with a sound phrase that is different from the phrase being
sung, but fits with it in some way. The new phrase can be a harmony
part, a rhythmic part, or can fill in a gap of silence.

The two singers continue their phrases, and the person sitting next
to the second singer joins in with a phrase that fits in some way with the
sounds already being made. And you progress around the circle, each
person offering a sound phrase until all the participants are sounding.

After a minute or two or three, the first singer drops out; and
then after a few bars, the second singer drops out; and then, after a
few bars, the third singer drops out; and so on until the last singer to
have entered is the only singer remaining. She continues her lone
phrase for a few bars before coming to a finish.

While a group might be skilled and take to this practice immediately, the ensemble tuning tends to improve with repeated efforts. So
don't worry if cacophony breaks loose for a couple of rounds. There
are two ways to regard cacophony: one is that the participants are not
listening carefully so when they join in, the sound phrases they offer
are not based on what they are hearing. If we listen carefully we tend
to add elements that enhance rather than detract from the whole. Second, modern and postmodern music includes dissonance and chaos,
which in the past have been considered unmusical. If your group creates a composition of dissonant and random patterns of sound, you
might consider viewing the work in a postmodern light.

Guidelines that might prove helpful:

1. Rather than attempting to be creative and unique in an effort to make a sound that will be noticed so that you will receive acclaim for your great inventiveness, be simple and easy and obvious.
2. If someone is making a sound phrase that pleases you, feel free to join in by making a similar phrase, changing only a single element.
3. Listen, listen, listen.

Work Play

People connect when they work together. Building a sand castle, cooking a meal, painting a mural, or digging beds in the garden, we find ways to cooperate and our opinions about politics, childrearing, or who God is have little relevance. The work enables us to find common ground.

A chef friend of mine is often invited to parties not to cook, but to supervise the cooking. Guests are given aprons and sharp knives, and my friend provides the raw materials and the recipes. I have had the honor of being invited to one of these gatherings, and as I chopped mushrooms and sauteed onions, I experienced none of the anxiety I often have when I go to a party and know none of the guests. Cooking together took the edge off, broke the ice, gave us something to do that we could talk about.

Inspired by this experience, I gave a latke party last Hanukkah. I invited my friends to bring big bowls and graters and everyone sat around shredding potatoes. People complained that their arms were tired, couldn't we please use the Cuisinart, but I didn't succumb. I knew that the potato pancakes would taste better if everyone had sweat a bit to make them, and that the atmosphere in the room would benefit. The effort paid off. By the time we lit the Hanukkah candles, the room felt warm and friendly, and the ritual reflected this intimacy. As they left, people thanked me not only for the latkes, but also for the ambience.

Here are a few ideas for group projects. Do whatever appeals to you from the list, and make up your own.

The Practice

When you're throwing a dinner party, have your guests draw the tablecloth. Spread butcher paper over the table and hand out colored felt-tip pens. Instead of having your guests draw discrete images, invite them to make patterns that interact with each other so that you're all participating in an overall design. Then set the table together.

Build a sculpture on the beach out of whatever you find: driftwood, shells, buoys, tires, seaweed.

Decorate a Christmas tree with homemade ornaments.

When you have a big project like painting your walls or digging beds in the garden, invite your friends to a work party. Put on music and dance during your breaks. Sing while you work.

Gather friends to make seasonal gifts: jam, pies, sachets, candles.

Gather friends for social activism: make food for the hungry, write letters to congresspeople, collect books for prison libraries, make baby blankets for homeless shelters.

Costume Party

During our summer retreat, my students and I spend an evening in character, dining in candlelight under a grape arbor in the garden. Everyone takes on a different voice, an altered physical style, an invented personal narrative, and stays in character for hours. As the evening wears on and the interactions become more complex, the delight thickens.

One year, Melanie donned a sheet and came as a sheik; Jaimie draped himself in a long skirt, hooked his hand around the sheik's elbow, and declared he was the favorite wife. Ashley pulled on a pair of thigh-gripping bell-bottoms and a wig of long curls and decided he was a Russian rock star. Pregnant Maria pushed a stroller full of debris and became a raving bag lady. Mel dressed up like a chicken and cackled all night.

Oddly enough, even though I have done this many times and have invariably enjoyed the transformation, each time I balk. "I don't waaaant to put on a costume," I bemoan in a back room where no one can hear me, while all my students are thrashing around in piles of clothing being dutifully inventive. "I can't figure out who to beeeeee," I whine to my assistant if I have one handy. "I haaaaate this game," I confide to the insects clinging to the ceiling as I finally manage to throw on some combination of clothing—a kimono hanging on a hook in the bathroom, a sequined dress in the back of the closet—and land on a character (an aging geisha with a popcorn fetish, a teetotalling flapper). As the evening goes on, my character becomes enlivened through her exchanges with the others until midnight arrives and my students retire to their beds and I am left bereft because I have lost all desire to return to normal reality.

What makes this practice fun is the relationships that develop between the characters. We often interact with each other in such repetitive ways that we are able to anticipate one another's every response. When we change character, the interpersonal dynamics transform and we awaken into a new life.

We are not who we think we are—we are not what we do, we are not our age, we are not our gender or sexual preference. We are not where we live or where we were born or what religion we were born into or went on to practice. We are not our skin color. We are not our bodies. We are not our thoughts. We are something that is unnamable, indescribable, vital, mysterious, and elementally free. We have known this truth since we first looked into a mirror when we were children and, surprised by our reflection, thought, *But that is not who I am.* All of our lives, we have looked into mirrors, startled by our reflections. *But that is not who I am,* we think in secret as we brush on mascara or shave our chins. And we are right. Yet we begin to believe we are who we have invented ourselves to be: the man in the dark blue suit with the striped tie and tasseled loafers, the woman in Birkenstocks with her long hair pulled up in a turquoise barrette. And not only do we fix ourselves in solid and false identities, we fix one another: he is the gay accountant in a pink cashmere sweater; she is the straight divorcée in pearl earrings who carries a Chanel purse and drives a gold Lexus.

We dress in costumes every day and night of our lives: formal and informal costumes, sexy costumes and power costumes, feminine costumes and masculine costumes, baggy costumes and fitted costumes, spring, summer, fall, and winter costumes, costumes that suit our age and culture and subculture. We have hair styles and shoe styles and eyebrow styles and we have fur styles for our pets. We have costumes for our furniture and our windows and our doors and all of these styles remind us of who we think we are. We have become so accustomed to using our outfits as a way to define and communicate our identity, that when we transform our dress, we invite an unordinary persona to emerge, and this coming out can be surprisingly liberating.

We can play with our lives, loosening the imprint of society and family and class and profession that demands we become who we are not and that we believe the falsification. We can be whoever we want to be, for an evening, an afternoon, a day, an hour—even a few minutes can be remarkably refreshing—and then return to our familiar identities. They will be waiting, ready for us to adopt them whenever we feel the need.

The Practice

Throw a costume party. You can invite your friends to arrive already in costume or provide a collection of clothes and hats and fabric and paraphernalia, ready when they arrive. Invite your guests to invent a character that grows out of the assembled costume rather than trying to be a famous character from history or Hollywood. Encourage the participants to imagine the life story and current situation of the character who emerges. For example, a cocktail waitress might have been married three times but is currently single and is craving a cigarette because this morning she quit smoking. A dog trainer might have just retired after being mauled by a pitt bull and she's looking for a new career. A surfer might be heading for Australia and wondering if anyone knows someone there who might put him up for a few weeks.

You can invite guests to come for afternoon tea and ask them to wear hats and gloves. My guests have shown up in sombreros, bicycle helmets, surgeon's bonnets, and cooking mitts, as well as white kid gloves and pillbox hats. I provide extra hats and gloves for guests who might have forgotten theirs or want to change style midparty.

You can ask people to bring costumes from their closets and at the party, each can choose among what is offered.

Whatever you do, remember: even as you don your costume, a part of you might not feel at all like exerting the effort, but in the end, you will be happy that you did.

Drumming

Last year, my friend Barbara Borden, who is a master percussionist, led a drumming circle for my birthday. She arrived at my studio early and set out her collection of drums and rattles and claves. I pulled out my conga drum and the basket of percussion instruments I had gathered over the years—shakers from Ecuador and the Amazon, tambourines from São Paulo, bone instruments from Mexico. We lit candles and set chairs out in a circle and at eight o'clock, guests began streaming in with their own rattles and drums.

Barbara began by inviting all of us to join her in a steady four-count beat, bringing her palm down firmly on the skin of her *djembe,* and we joined in, all of us in the most simple unison, drumming out the beat. She then taught different rhythms to each arc of the circle, the sound thickening and thinning and syncopating and thrumming. We beat our drums and shook our rattles, and as we relaxed, the rhythm settled into a steadiness that carried itself, that held time but took us out of time, rhythm strong and layered and moving, a train of rhythm taking us somewhere together.

As the time passed, marked by our drumming, we entered a different state of mind together, a trance together. I could feel the change and see it in the eyes and the bodies of my friends. We kept going, drumming, holding the beat steady, as Barbara took off on her drum, flying with rhythm, her hands strong and confident, the beat happening through her without thought—if you stop to figure it out, you are lost, the beat is lost, the circle crumbles. We held the ground for Barbara so that she could take us with her into flight, and I looked around the circle and smiles were breaking out like small fires. We were more than happy, unless what you call happy includes a grace note of grief, because I could see the sorrow, too, in the eyes and the smiles. The divorces, the brothers and lovers lost to AIDS, the sisters and wives and mothers lost to breast cancer, the parents and grandparents lost to age—the host of disappointments that set up housekeeping in the heart despite how often wisdom delivers eviction notices. By drumming we had, together, lifted off the ground so that the angle of the view was wide and held the panorama within its frame without flinching. And we kept on drumming.

If you put clocks in a room that have pendulums swinging at different rhythms, within a day or two, the pendulums will be moving in unison. Scientists call this tendency of objects and beings to modulate rhythms in order to achieve unison with each other "entrainment." Our bodies are rhythmic organisms: our hearts beat in response to electrical impulses and a pulse moves through our veins. We breathe in rhythms, walk in rhythms, jog in rhythms, talk in rhythms; and when we walk or jog or talk with another, we tend to entrain our pace with that of our partner. We live in a rhythmic universe: the earth rotates around the sun and the moon around the earth at steady rhythms that affect the internal rhythms of our bodies—the patterns of biochemicals, of waking and sleep—and affect the rhythms of the planetary waters rising and falling, and the rhythms of the seasons. When we drum together, we entrain, establishing a connection with each other, and together, shaking rattles and slapping the skin of drums with our bare and reddened palms, we connect to the rhythmic universe.

Hearing the connection that we are making through the rhythm played by our hands, we bond with one another, and when we feel the bonding occur, the connection deepens so that it is no longer a mechanical connection but an energetic one, as if the rhythm that is being birthed by our hands is itself driving our hands.

Rhythm delivers us from our sense of individual and separate self into the felt sensation of the collective. By establishing a pulse, we are not only entraining our hands, but also our hearts and minds. Despite our wishes, struggles continue to arise, misunderstandings abound, conflicts driven by clashing needs erupt. Peace is not a steady state, but must be created over and over again. If we are interested in healing the rifts within our own hearts, in building community, in alleviating our suffering and that of others, we can find a common rhythm and beat it out, together.

The Practice

Gather a group together and a collection of percussion instruments. If you and your friends do not own drums or rattles, you can make them. Fill empty jars with beans or pebbles, bring out a washboard, chopsticks, wooden spoons, wooden bowls, pots and pans, plastic water bottles. Sit in a circle.

The leader begins playing a simple pulse that everyone can follow. Play that pulse in unison until the beat is firmly established and then add other rhythmic patterns while at least one person holds the simple ground pulse.

If, as you are playing, the rhythm falls apart, stop and begin again with a clear unison beat.

Drum until you reach an organic stopping place. Then rest, and begin again, taking the time to establish a clear pulse before adding other rhythms to the mix.

eight

Enlivening Love

The Sacred Play of Passion

"To love is to tilt with the lightning, two bodies routed by a single honey's sweet."

—PABLO NERUDA

(Translated by Terence Clarke)

Imagination Climbs into Bed

"There is nothing more exhilarating than being creative about how to love . . . The secret to your success is not to do what he [or she] would expect, but to step outside the box and go to a place you've never been before."

LOU PAGET

Our lovemaking experiences are in part physical and in part imaginative. By imaginative, I am not referring to whom we might be fantasizing about while we are embracing a partner, but how, because of the content of our minds, we can be deeply aroused by a lover's touch one moment, and the next day be left cold by the same lover stroking us in precisely the same manner. Sex has a little to do with our rational minds and a lot to do with primal urges, early conditioning, and the stories we tell ourselves, often without the clarity of awareness. Spontaneous games and rituals invite the personalities, archetypes, and energies that live submerged to expose themselves on the playing field and transform the bedroom into the ground of holy fun.

Erotic excitement is heightened by the unpredictable, but while most of us long for novelty, many of us are wary of introducing new games into our tried and true relationships. We might experiment with an exotic new position or dress in leopard-spotted translucent lingerie and fishnet stockings for a secret liaison, but for an evening with our long-term partner?—even the idea can bring a blush of embarrassment howling across the cheeks. The introduction of games and rituals into the bedroom may require a mustering of mettle, but even a timid adventure into new ground pays large rewards.

The value of this chapter lies in the spirit of the practices. Playfulness and invocations of the sacred lend a dimension to lovemaking that no technical savvy can replace. Amusement is one of the most profound and least discussed aspects of love—the ability to laugh at our hungers and fears, confusion and cellulite, odors and scars, grunts and spinach between the teeth. All the great sages I have had the fortune to meet have had a twinkle in their eyes. Despite having witnessed great human suffering, they continue to be amused by this odd, wonderful, and fleeting life and their lightness of being is contagious. In their presence, I, too, break into a smile that would glow in the dark. Life can evoke a good belly laugh, and a great orgasm, if we have the wherewithal to remember how to amuse ourselves.

But pleasure and amusement are not the only benefits that are derived from bedroom play. When our passion is ignited and we are able to express ourselves freely in the act of love, we experience deep intimacy. As we emerge from our hiding places and let what is within us out, we come to know one another more thoroughly, to appreciate one another more fully, to fall in love with one another, and the world, again and again and again.

Preparing the Space

Jack lived only blocks away from the roaring freeway in a neighborhood of run-down homes, dilapidated warehouses, and vacant lots strewn with trash. I had to walk through rubble to get to the front door. As I stood alone on the sidewalk and rang the doorbell, waiting to hear his feet clump-clump down the stairs, I wondered what in the world I was doing. And then I stepped inside and any doubt that had arisen about my choice of lovers instantly evaporated. One evening, a trail of single red tulips in small vases led to a bed circled by candlelight. Another night, the space was in total darkness except for the clawfoot tub, luminescent with bubbles. I couldn't stay away. I loved the way he made things look.

The bedroom is the theater of love. In part, what we love about theater is the fantasy, and the fantasy is made believable by the set. As a story unfolds on stage, we enter a time and place of the imagination, and at the same time we remain audience members sitting shoulder to shoulder in a darkened room. In this act of simultaneity, we enter a different life without giving up the one we already have—and we like that. We like simultaneity in the bedroom as well. Our libido kicks in when we are allowed to be someone other than who we are and somewhere other than where we are, while we stay ourselves and remain in the bedroom.

In Rajasthan, I visited a palace where the raj had commissioned a different artisan to design each of the myriad rooms. The walls of the prayer room were covered with tiny mirrors set several inches apart so that when candles were lit the flames would refract, multiplying into thousands of shimmering lights. I tried to imagine what the praying people had felt like in the center of a gazillion flames, and I thought about how the artisan was crafting not only the look of a space but also working with the way light changes the way we feel. Paying attention to light is important because of this very issue—light affects not only how we see, but how we feel.

And then there is food.

It was New Year's morning and I was in a Japanese hotel in San Francisco with a man I had noticed was attractive the moment I set eyes on him. After a week of talking to one another during dinners and forest walks, we had decided to spend the night together before he flew home, and there we lay. He reached for the futon-side phone, ordered a plate of fresh fruit from room service, and when it arrived, he picked up a strawberry and fed me a bite and then slipped the remaining half into his own mouth. I was lit with mad and blinding love (the taste of strawberry lingering on my tongue, the crunch of tiny golden seeds alive between my molars) as I watched the juicy red heart with my very own teeth marks on it slide into his mouth and disappear. Each piece of watermelon, pineapple, mango, was an erotic wonder. While I do not recommend falling hopelessly in love with a man who is about to return to his home thousands of miles away, I do fully recommend attending to the Eros of taste by setting offerings of food here and there—chocolates, champagne, apricot juice, oysters, mangoes, profiteroles—and at some moment during your tryst, fully indulging.

Later that New Year's morning, when my friend put on his clothes, he lingered for a while in his undershirt—one of those plain white cotton sleeveless ones with deep cuts around the armpits that direct the eye to the muscular bulge of pectorals and upper arm—and I understood for the first time why God created men's underwear. We all might as well admit that we love bedroom costumes and go ahead and indulge: velvet bras, silk pajamas, boas, high-heeled mules, pink satin boxer shorts, a T-shirt with holes ready to be ripped off the body by teeth. We can pull out hats and hang them from the bedposts, or masks, or blindfolds, or prom dresses, or gloves, or knee socks, or high heels, or scarves, or fur coats, or aprons, or kilts.

And then there is music.

My friend Jim was a performance artist. He loved puns. He gave me a set of music boxes he had made out of tin spice boxes. The chile played "La Cucaracha." He lived in a loft in San Francisco. The only pieces of furniture in the bedroom were two speakers and a mattress, and before we climbed into bed Jim would set up the play list. One night he played Steve Reich's "Drumming," a thirty-minute piece of pure rhythm that starts off slow and simple and then builds, one layer at a time, until it's hard and driving, and your head is in a totally different state from when the music started. You're not sure how you got there but you're glad you did. One night he played singing saws, another night zydeco, another night music that his friends had composed for computer and garbage can. The music affected the way we rolled around so we kept discovering different ways of doing things in bed. We rocked in that loft.

Sometimes you don't want music, you just want the sounds of breath and grunt and sigh and murmur and yelps and growls and the occasional howl. But other times, you want music, the same way you want music for dancing. Music changes the way you feel and feeds energy straight into the body, and when you both listen to the same music, your bodies get in sync and the mind surrenders and sensations race into the space that thought has abandoned, and that feels good.

The Practice

Preparing a room for the act of love can be as simple as changing the lighting. A director friend of mine lined the baseboards of his house with votive candles—very religious and sexy. Draping the bedposts with strings of Christmas lights turns the bed into a carnival, although you might want to be careful not to end up tangled in cords; on the other hand, being tangled up in Christmas lights might be precisely the way to go. Or simply place a soft-colored bulb in a bedside light and the whole room will feel different. Or go all out and hang a disco ball from the ceiling and plug in a strobe.

But what are we illuminating? Usually a room that we sleep in night after night, the shape and contours so familiar, we can find our way to the bathroom in the dark and reach for the alarm clock with our eyes closed. While this level of comfort is conducive to a certain ease in daily life, it is not particularly favorable for erotic play. Eros responds to the way things look. Cover the top of the dresser with green apples, or pumpkins lit from within, or bowls of water filled with floating candles and gardenias. Line the edges of the room with stones, blanket the floor with fall leaves, sprinkle the bed with rose petals, hang feathers within reach. Instead of a single item go for multiples—vases of single roses on bookshelves and bureaus and windowsills and bedside tables and ledges and stairways and bathroom counters. Have fun.

Use your imagination. Use what is at hand. Take advantage of the season. Take five minutes, or ten, or fifteen, and devote yourself to making the space an erotic playground.

Oils, Ablutions, and Blessings

Recently over dinner, a friend of mine told me about his new girlfriend. "The first time we made love," he said, "she kneeled in front of me and took off my clothes, one item at a time, folding them at my feet. She didn't say anything." He paused and I noticed tears in his eyes. "I had never felt so honored," he confessed. My friend had been sexually abused as a child and until that moment, when his lover knelt before him as though in worship and slowly disrobed him to reveal his nakedness, he had never experienced his body as something deserving of reverence.

All of us forget that our bodies deserve our esteemed regard and instead treat them like indentured servants. *Shut up,* we tell our lower backs which ache due to sitting longer hours than humans were designed to. *I can't believe you have the gall to complain given how much extremely important work we have to get done. Here, I'll give you an aspirin. Now shape up.* So we need to remind ourselves and each other by ablutions and anointings that this mortal body of flesh and bone is holy, holy, holy.

I attended a ritual with a shaman from Ecuador, famous for his singing of prayers. He set up an altar and then began chanting into a bottle, singing hard, calling on the spirits for their assistance, praying them into the water that he had steeped with aromatic flowers from the rainforest. He continued to chant into the bottle as he sprinkled us, and while there may be no scientific evidence supporting the fact that singing prayers into fluid changes the chemical nature of the substance, I could feel the effect, those droplets sweet as French perfume showering my head with blessings. I felt good. I felt blessed.

When we do ritual acts with the body, we affect the heart and the mind. In order to move our minds out of the living room world of headline news and mail-order catalogs and the leftover half of a peanut butter and jelly sandwich in our kid's lunchbox, and into the bedroom world of sacred toes and godly navels, we benefit from a transitional aid. By enacting a physical ritual we give a message, through the body to the subconscious, that we are shifting modes, and in this way we prepare for our love to be not only a bodily pleasure, but also a romp through the land of the spirits. And we don't have to rely on imported shamans; we can bless and anoint each other.

The Practice

Remove each other's clothing one item at a time. Fill a bath with herbs and flowers from the garden. Spray lavender water or rose water on hot faces and bottoms of feet. Rub naked skin with scented lotion. Light a bundle of dried sage and waft the smoke over each other's bodies. And all the while bless all and everything.

Blessings do not need to be complicated or even creative, just uttered. A classical Buddhist wish for well-being is quite straightforward, time tested, and effective: "May you be happy, may you be peaceful." Wishes for peace and happiness are always a good place to begin. Then make up your own blessings and wishes for your lover.

Gratitude is a good heart softener. Say what you appreciate about your lover. "I am grateful for your biceps," she says. "I am grateful for the smell of your skin," he says. "I am grateful for your smile," she says. "I am grateful for the mole between your breasts," he says and kisses her on that dark spot. Go beyond physical characteristics into quirky aspects of one another's being. "I love how you laugh like a duck," she says. "I love how you tilt your head to the side and pucker your lips when you're trying to understand directions," he says.

Giving and receiving wishes for well-being and naming what delights us can arouse profound feelings of love and gratitude as we remember how much we care for one another. When sensual pleasure and authentic love are so intertwined as to be inseparable, we become what the holy texts promise: gods and goddesses in a divine embrace.

We must be on guard, however, for the deadly danger of

overearnestness and call on the spirits of the absurd and the ridiculous. Be silly. Be inventive. Be playful. Be irreverent. Caress each other with the feathers of raptors and the soft tips of weeds. Shake rattles around each other's bodies that you make from aspirin bottles and matchbooks. Draw symbols on breasts and buttocks and foreheads with whipped cream. Lick eyelids. Kiss toe tips. Tickle ribs. Turn condoms into puppets as you call on the spirits of Eros and laughter.

An Artful Touch

I was in Zagreb a few years ago to give a performance at an international dance festival and my friend Malena, whose boyfriend was out of town for a couple of weeks, insisted I move into her apartment—a large front room, a minuscule alcove kitchen, and a tiny bathroom, where to sit on the toilet you had to turn sideways so your knees wouldn't bump into the wall. Each night, Malena and I pulled a futon from the closet, made the bed on the floor, and as the war still raged on the shifting borders in the far distance, we lay awake under the covers discussing, often heatedly, the complex politics of the Balkans until we were bleary-eyed with exhaustion. Then we launched into confidences about our love lives.

Malena, who has flawless olive skin and thick black hair and gypsy blood, had known her boyfriend for a couple of years before they fell in love—they were part of a circle of friends who had gone to film school together, and every night they gathered at the club down the street from Malena's apartment. One night, she was sitting with her friends on a stone wall across from the club, dangling her legs and smoking a cigarette. Boric nestled in beside her. As the conversation bounced around from their work with CNN on the war front to the fantasies they had of moving to Amsterdam, Boric gently traced a circle around Malena's ankle.

"I wish he would touch me like that again," Malena whispered, lying beside me in the dark, the glow of her cigarette illuminating her dark eyes. "We have been together two years and it seems he has forgotten the subtleties of love."

Subtle and intelligent touch can awaken, and reawaken love. If we pay attention, the body has an architecture and when we are touched in a way that traces this design, we feel that we are being touched by intelligent hands that are coming to know us and at the same time, telling us who we are. As the awareness of our own structure awakens—the way our bones fit together and our muscles lie against bone, the way our bellies slope and breasts curve and noses jut and toes emerge from pad of foot—we experience a sensual well-being. We can pleasure one another by tracing what is there, by drawing the body just as it is.

The Practice

Trace your partner's skeleton, feeling the bones under your fingers, their shape and the way they meet one another. Draw the spine, the shoulder blades, the pelvis, the ribs, the limbs, the fingers, the toes.

Trace the curves of the body, outlining the eyes, the lips, the breasts, the belly, the buttocks. Come to know the angles, the juts, the promontories, the hollows. Let the fingers gather information about muscle, and bone, and the rivers of vein and artery. We are each extraordinary works of art. Touch brings us into awareness about the shape of our bodies, guides consciousness into the sensations of the body, awakens the pure sensuality of being alive in a body.

Take five minutes or ten or one. Each time we touch with a listening hand, we soothe, care, and love.

Receiving touch is generally quite enjoyable, but *giving* touch can feel like work. What makes touching pleasurable is an element of play, novelty, and experimentation. We can invent spontaneous patterns of touch in the same way we make a painting—drawing lines, spirals, circles, triangles on our lover's clothed or naked body. We can make long strokes, short strokes, thin strokes with the tip of a finger, broad strokes with the flat of the hand. We can find strokes for the soles of the feet, the eyelids, the buttocks, the knees.

I am often surprised at how effective even a minute of careful touch can be, how my mood can be transformed, my spirit calmed, my sense of well-being enhanced. As you sit with your lover on the couch reading the newspaper, pause for a moment and stroke his arm with a listening attention, knowing the beauty of arm.

Contact

Yani Novak, one of my dance colleagues in the late seventies, invited friends to her San Francisco loft one afternoon to experiment with a form of movement improvisation she called boko maru. Yani told us to pick a partner and then gave instructions in the ritual washing of feet. Taking turns, we lay our partner's naked toes in a bucket of warm and frothy water, scrubbed soles, massaged ankles, caressed arches, and dried wet skin with warm towels. Next, Yani told us to lie on our backs with the shining soles of our feet pressed up against the soles of our partner's feet. Whenever we felt the impulse to move, we were to follow that impulse and maintain physical contact as our movement developed.

I remember the comfort of the beginning: soles pressed against soles, nerve endings warm and buzzing. And then, the first crawl of movement, a toe sliding toward an ankle, the ball of a foot tucked into an arch. Then, my feet inching up my partner's legs as her feet inched up mine until we found ourselves rolling. I remember lying on my partner's back as she crawled across the floor; and later, her body pressed against my back as I carried her, her weight a heavy pleasure. And finally, when Yani asked us to find an ending, how only the tips of our fingers touched, the movement slow and quiet but looming inside consciousness like the bold light of the moon as it crests a hill and showers the night sky. I remember afterward how full I felt from the luxury of so much touch, how satisfied.

A year later, Steve Paxton showed up at my studio in downtown Oakland and taught contact improvisation. Again I found myself nestled up against bodies, rolling and flopping over backs, dancing for hours moved only by shifting points of physical contact. A door into a universe of touch and movement and play had been flung open.

Contact is a form of dancing built entirely on touch. Two people meet head to head, or hand to hand, or shoulder to shoulder, or hip to hip, and from the point of contact, movement emerges. The task of the dancers is to maintain physical connection while the dance flows from movement to movement. Skilled contact dancers work quite vigorously, lifting and tossing and catching one another with an impressive gymnastic virtuosity. And because of its sensual joy and unpredictability, contact improvisation is still thriving decades after its inception.

When studying contact improvisation, many preliminary exercises are offered to learn to flow from touch and to bear weight, and all of them are enjoyable whether or not one ever goes on to full-out contact dancing. When I offer the following exercises in my workshops, after a minute of nervous giggling and whispering, a silence takes hold of the room as the focus shifts from the mind to the body. The body knows what to do, knows what feels good, and delights in our surrender to the call for touch.

Engaging with our love partner in practices that are physically intimate but not explicitly erotic, we expand the territory of our pleasures. By investigating the range of possibilities for touch, when we do find ourselves in bed, we will have cultivated an entirely new vocabulary of love.

The Practice

HAND CONTACT

Stand facing your partner, close your eyes, and let your hands touch. Allow movement to arise from the touch of fingers and palm, and begin by moving only the hands.

As you continue, allow the point of contact to move up the lower arm to the upper arm, and then continue up to the shoulder. If you are working easily with flow, let the point of contact continue to shift, moving to the back and the head. Experiment with letting your body weight lean into your partner as her weight leans into you.

Begin this work with utmost ease, and build one step at a time. Let the contact be what dances you, and work until you are ready to come to an end.

BOKO MARU

A lovely way to begin boko maru is to wash one another's feet, massaging ankles and arches and toes, but if time is an issue, rinse and dry your own feet quickly. Then, lie on your back with the soles of your bare feet touching the soles of your partner's feet. Rest for a minute in stillness. Whenever you feel an impulse to begin, move your feet while maintaining contact with your partner's feet. Follow the impulses that arise from the contact and, slowly, allow the contact to move to other parts of the body. Go wherever you go, which might be nowhere at all. Be puppies, be seals, be kittens, be human. Enjoy the contact.

I traveled with my father last year to the Galapagos Islands. At many of the sites where we disembarked, herds of seals lounged on the dark and crusty volcanic rock of the shore. They did not lie alone, but slung and slouched over one another. We humans clustered around them, sighing as we pulled out our cameras to savor the images of snuggling bodies for a future look. In the seals, we saw ourselves, our own very human, very animal nature.

Natural Décor

While doing research for an opera she was composing, my friend Sylvia Nakaach learned of a courting ritual enacted by the women of an Amazonian tribe. If interested in a man, a woman asks him to meet her at night at a designated place in the rainforest. To prepare for the rendezvous, she collects luminescent leaves and plasters them to her skin. Serenaded by the drone of insects, she emerges from the tangle of vines, her naked body glowing in the dark. An irresistible seduction.

The fact that we can be aroused by the way a body is adorned sends throngs of people scurrying to malls, fuels the publication of countless magazines, employs masses of underpaid underage seamstresses and overpaid anorexic models, and propels us to rummage for hours through our closets in an often disappointing effort to dress ourselves in a style that will enchant the evening's company. We dress and adorn to seduce. We cut our hair, pierce our ears, navels, nipples, tattoo our thighs, biceps, buttocks to seduce. We paint on makeup and don hats and slip our feet into spike heels and platform shoes and polished loafers to seduce. And we drape and bind ourselves in bright ties, garter belts, teddies, corsets, silk boxer shorts, Miracle Bras—to seduce, all the while forgetting that there are ways to play with the Eros of body decor which do not require a trip to the mall or local tattoo parlor or a bout of midnight e-shopping. Like the women in the Amazon, we can use what is freely given to adorn our bodies.

The Practice

Go outside with a basket or a paper bag and collect whatever pleases you: leaves, branches, feathers, stones, flowers, grasses, berries, shells, driftwood, sand. If you are in the city, go to a park, or snip flowers from your planter boxes. Then, find a nesting spot where you won't be disturbed, indoors or outdoors, where you can be warm and private.

Decorate your lover's body with whatever you have collected. Perhaps you will lay a line of stones down the center of your partner's body—one on the forehead, one over the heart, one on the solar plexus, one in the middle of the belly. You might place a flat, cool leaf over each eye or sprinkle flower petals over breasts or entwine a sprig of berries to crown the hair.

Adorn your lover's body in a way that pleases and amuses you, as if you were making art. Add color here, texture there, find patterns that enhance the curves and lines and erotic nature of your partner's body—a circle around breasts, a line to the pubis, a buttercup around the belly button.

I was taking a walk through the woods near my house with my friend Fred one afternoon. I had recently broken up from a seven-year relationship and, although I knew Fred had a romantic interest in me, I was not particularly drawn to him and I was determined to stay single. We settled down to rest on the side of a hill, under a sprawling oak tree with a view of Mount Tamalpais. I have no recollection of what we talked about, but what I do remember is that the day was warm and I was wearing shorts, and that Fred picked a forget-me-not from the field of grasses where we sat and held it for several minutes, twirling it in his fingers. Then, as if casually, he stroked my leg with the blue flower. He made no other physical overtures that afternoon. In fact, it was weeks before we kissed. But on the hillside, I had known in a terrifying instant that we would become lovers. I could not resist the touch of the flower.

The Practice (continued)

As you practice with natural decor, pay attention to the way you imagine each object feels when it is laid on your partner's body so that you are attending to the received sensations. A cool leaf on each eyelid will relax the eyes. A pile of pebbles on the lower belly will soften the abdominal wall.

Find the sensitive parts of the body that enjoy soft touch—the inner thighs, the backs of the knees, the neck, the breasts, the soles of the feet, the belly—and stroke these parts with a feather or a flower or a soft grass or a warm stone.

One summer when I was teaching a workshop on Mel and Su's land, we discovered that if we ground the soft river stones against a hard rock, we could make a colored paste. For hours we painted each other's faces. What surprised me was not only how much delight we aroused by the transformation of our appearance, but also how much we each enjoyed the feeling of having our faces painted—the sensual pleasure of cool stone mush stroked across cheek and brow and eyelid.

Make colored paste from leaves and flowers and river stones. Or paint your lover's body with chocolate syrup, colored frosting, whipped cream, and pomegranate seeds.

Tribal peoples, sophisticated in the use of body decor for the purposes of ritual, rely on the transformation of the physical body to enter altered states of consciousness in order to heal and hunt and commune with the spirits of animals and plants. If we regard lovemaking as a spiritual practice that involves a transformation of consciousness, we can be aided by techniques that alter the way we habitually perceive. The visual transformation of the body is a tool for gaining entry into nonordinary realms of being and once there, we find ourselves behaving in nonordinary ways.

Location Scouting

One night, midkiss, Fred leapt up from my sofa and started moving the furniture. I had only known him a few weeks and thought of him as a reserved computer nerd who wore dark-rimmed glasses and a plastic pocket liner to protect his shirts from ink stains. I watched, unamused, as he shoved a small table against a wall to clear a pathway and started pushing my couch across the room. He refused to explain to me what he had in mind and as I stood pressed into a corner making room for his antics, I began composing Dear John letters in my head: *I've really enjoyed your company, but . . .* Fred settled the sofa directly in front of the fireplace, lit an instant log, and rolled me onto the couch. As we embraced in the glow of the fire, Fred rose to new heights in my esteem—the location was excellent.

One Sunday afternoon, a few weeks later, Fred abandoned me midembrace and disappeared into the backyard. I found him with a chaise lounge pad in his arms, which he carried from its wooden frame on the brick patio over to a patch of grass lined with iris and settled me down in the sun-drenched garden. He pulled a bottle of scented massage oil out of his pocket and commanded that I be still as he caressed my body in the garden. I gave up thinking about him as a reserved man who wore a pocket liner.

One night, just as our passion began to heat up, Fred ran across the room and scurried halfway up the ladder to my loft, beckoning me to follow. We kissed in a precarious embrace, dangling over the tile floor, and then he scampered down the ladder and under the dining table. We chased each other around the house for an hour, ending up in novel embraces as interesting as any *Kama Sutra* pose. The moment the heat climbed to the point where one or the other of us began to melt into submission, the other one would dash off to a new location—the bathtub, under the redwood tree, on our knees beneath the dining table—until finally an embrace so took us that we both surrendered.

Where we are affects *how* we are. Often at the beginning of a love relationship, mutual passion is so great that we find ourselves half-naked on the floor or backed up against the kitchen wall. The novelty of the situation unleashes us, we move into lovemaking uncensored. Unfortunately, we cannot develop satisfying long-term relationships if we continually seek fresh romance. Fortunately, we don't have to rely on the sizzle of newly kindled romance to enjoy the pleasure of novel locations.

The Practice

Prepare a nest for romance. You can either do this in advance of your tryst, or surprise your lover midkiss and dash off to a new place. Take the couch with you, or a soft blanket, light a fire or a candle, have a pillow or two handy. You can make a sanctuary in an alcove, or if it's warm outside, make a bed in the garden. You don't need to go to the Ritz or the wine country to have an exciting spot for a rendezvous— make one next to your rosebush, or in the kitchen, or on your balcony.

Remember, while you can prepare a spot in advance of a tryst, you can also rely on the inspiration of the moment. Pull back from a hot embrace and lead your lover somewhere. Slide under the kitchen table or dive behind the couch or flip on the shower.

What can be difficult about moving from the bedroom to the terrace is not the walk from one place to another, but the mental movement. We long to be more inventive in our love lives, yet we hesitate to invent. Making an agreement with a spouse or lover to add the element of play can help us feel permission to actually act on our impulses, rather than dismiss them. Making a commitment to ourselves to enliven our love lives is also helpful. Commitment works in mysterious ways. Once we say to ourselves we are going to find a new place to kiss our lover, we do not have to work at carrying out the action—the impulse will arise spontaneously and we will find ourselves by the water in a luscious embrace, below a crescent moon.

Character Play

At seven-thirty on a Friday evening, my friend Mark and I headed to a party in the East Bay. As we had feared, the freeway was clogged with weekend traffic. Mark is British and since I'm an actress and unable to restrain myself, I began to imitate his accent. Instead of bonking me on the head and reprimanding me for being garishly rude, Mark launched into a Cockney tongue and together we entered a conversation we would never have broached had we been talking in our normal voices.

"You're driving in the wrong bloody lane like you always do!" I railed. "You always find the slowest car on the thoroughfare and place yourself behind it for the whole bloody trip."

"Always complainin' ya are, always unhappy ya are, miserable ya are, always wanting to be in control," Mark griped.

"You're the one that wanted to go to the bloody party in the first place, always needing to go out and impress people."

"Naw, 'twas yer idea. Whatever ya ask, whatever ya want, I bloody do it for ya."

Continuing to inch our way through the clot of cars, we abandoned the English couple for a pair of Indian sages.

"Ah cha, how good to be still," Mark said bobbing his head back and forth and grinning.

"It is important not that we get there, only that we be here," I said with an Indian lilt and a head wiggle.

We leapt from character to character, adding gestures and facial expressions and bursts of emotion, expressing whatever came to our minds without pausing to assess if our words were appropriate or made sense or might offend.

When we finally arrived at the party, we realized we had to reinvoke our familiar personalities before going inside and could barely find our way back to our boring bland normal selves.

"I think the ride over will have been the best part of the evening," Mark groaned.

The second we strapped on our seat belts for the ride home, we launched into our characters again with the glee of adolescents finding themselves free of chaperones.

"You always drive so bloody slow," I whined.

"Complainin', complainin', ya damn well drive yerself the next time. See if I come round to get ya," Mark retorted.

I had known Mark for years, had always been fond of him, but that night when he dropped me off at home and I waved goodbye, I missed him instantly.

Play opens the heart and allows us to be less hidden with one another. Instead of being careful and protected and polite, we become unleashed and silly and wild, and the wildness inside is more truly who we are than the veneer of staid behavior we generally expose. When we feel permission to reveal our inner life—the characters that are impolite, or spouting cosmic wisdom, or angry, or flirtatious—and we witness each other exposed, we cannot help but appreciate each other's company.

The Practice

While you are with your partner—in the car, having dinner in a restaurant, having morning coffee—change your voice and continue to converse. You can talk in an accent (Southern, English, French, Spanish) or change the quality of your voice (a very high voice, a very low voice, a squeaky voice, a gruff voice). You can talk in the same accent (two Texans carrying on, or two French people) or you can talk in different voices (a person with a very gruff voice, and a person with a very sweet, flirtatious voice).

Allow the conversation to go where it goes. If you are unsatisfied with the voice you have chosen, change to another.

While this exercise may seem daunting, the real difficulty is not getting into character (which is easy once you give yourself permission to experiment), but returning to normal reality. In coming back to your ordinary voice, you might feel as though life is instantly desiccating. Don't worry. You can return to the playing field in an instant by altering your voice and letting the myriad characters that populate your inner world out of your mouth.

Take the game to bed. Strike up a conversation in character as you make love. Or sing as if you were in an opera (which we are, we just forget to sing). Or talk in French or Spanish or German or gibberish. Characters you had no idea were in you will scamper out. Perhaps you will find a persona you are particularly fond of and want to stay in character for a while. Go ahead. Perhaps you will tire of a persona and want to find another. Go ahead. Don't worry about planning in advance who you will become. Simply alter your voice in one way or another and let everyone escape from their closet of polite silence.

nine

Prayer

The Language of the Heart

Remember
That to have the eyes of an artist,
That can be enough,
The ear of a poet,
That can be enough.
The soul of a human
just pointed
in the direction of the divine,
that can be more than enough.
I tell you this to remind myself.
Every gesture is an act of creation.
Even empty spaces and silence
can be the wings and voices of angels.
—MICHELE LINFANTE

The Path to What Is Holy

I had the privilege recently of meeting a woman of great intellectual stature—the recipient of a MacArthur Fellowship, a Guggenheim Fellowship, and a Pulitzer Prize—at a writers' retreat. Undaunted by the fact that she was nearing her eightieth birthday, she still worked as a columnist for a prestigious newspaper and had just begun a biography of a renowned figure in her field. One afternoon, while we lunched together on the patio outside my room, she told me that she had wed when she was twenty-one, largely as a way of escaping from the stifling atmosphere of her parents' home, and that she had lived most of her life in a semireclusive state, devoting herself to her work and to her relationship. She attributed the success of her career to passion and the success of her marriage to luck—and she added that she and her husband were so close they did not need God.

But when her husband died from a debilitating disease, she found herself devoid of a spiritual practice at a time when she longed for support through a devastating grief. She hunted for a congregation to join, but found none, she said, because no religion or set of rituals existed that suited her nature. So she proceeded through her mourning and, no longer in crisis, abandoned her search for a spiritual practice.

After lunch, I returned to my room to write but my thoughts were occupied with this woman's story. I imagined she might again have an experience that would so sadden her, frighten her, or confuse her, that she would long for a way to address her spiritual needs. And in the event that such a yearning did arise, I wondered if she would find a style of prayer and meditation to address the calling of the soul, or if she would remain convinced that none existed. Sitting at my desk, I stared out the window at the sunlight dappling the surface of the lake, and thought about the many occasions I, also, had experienced an impulse to express the spiritual longings of my heart but did not give voice to the urge. Although I remembered prayers from my childhood and had learned chants and mantras from my many forays into shamanism, Buddhism,

Hinduism, and eclectic feather-waving, drum-beating ceremonies, for most of my life I felt timid about bursting into heart-gushing prayer on my own.

Eventually, the urge to pray grew stronger than my fear of praying and I began to experiment. I discovered that my car provided an ideal retreat for private investigations into prayer, particularly when parking was sparse. A friend had told me that the god of parking was named Squat, so I made up a prayer to him that I recited as I circled the city blocks. The melody demanded I sing a tad bit like Kiri Te Kanawa, which made driving around and around quite entertaining despite the lack of curbside space and the merciless passage of time. Without fail, after repeated incantations, an empty spot along the curb would appear, even in the parts of town that were infamous for instigating murderous rages over rare parking places.

Bolstered by the success of my supplications to Squat, I ventured further into the territory of spontaneous prayer, freeing my experiments from the confines of the driver's seat. I prayed while hiking in the woods, while working out in my studio, backstage before performances, lying in the bathtub, and recently, when I experienced a health crisis, I prayed in biopsy rooms and while strapped inside MRI machines. The more I played with prayer, the more satisfying, illuminating, and becalming the act of praying became.

On the last day of the writers' retreat, I visited my friend in her room to say goodbye. She stood leaning against the cherrywood desk where she had been writing all month, her makeup carefully applied, her clothing impeccably fitted, her suitcases locked and ready by the door. She told me how much she was looking forward to smelling the rose geraniums that grew on the windowsill of her Manhattan apartment. Lifting her fingers to her nose, she closed her eyes and drew in a long breath. "That aroma is magnificent," she said. A radiance filled her being and spread across the room to me; and there I sat, blessed by the phantom scent of rose geraniums. The power of the transmission was so visceral I recognized that while my friend had been unable to find a formal spiritual practice, she had discovered an inner path that led to equanimity, wonder, and appreciation.

It is this very inner state of being that Brother David Steindl-Rast calls true prayer. "Suppose, for example, you are reciting Psalms," he writes in *Gratefulness, the Heart of Prayer.* "If all goes well, this may be a truly prayerful experience. But all doesn't always go well. While reciting Psalms, you might experience nothing but a struggle against distractions. Half an hour later you are watering your African violets. Now, suddenly the prayerfulness that never came during the prayers overwhelms you. You come alive from within. Your heart expands and embraces those velvet leaves, the blossoms looking up to you. The watering and drinking become a give-and-take so intimate that you cannot separate your pouring of the water from the roots' receiving, the flower's giving of joy from your drinking it in. And in a rush of gratefulness your heart celebrates this belonging together. As long as this lasts, everything has meaning, everything makes sense. You are communicating with your full self, with all there is, with God. Which was the real prayer, the Psalms or the watering of your African violets?"

Prayer in its deepest sense is not a recitation of liturgy, or a request for a parking place, or even a supplication for healing—although prayer can be all and any of these. Prayer in its deepest sense is the heart finding the path to its natural state of peace, wisdom, and compassion.

For those times in our lives when our intellect is unable to provide condolence to a heart that is sundered with grief, or provide clarity to a mind obscured by confusion and fear, we turn to spiritual practice. Prayer is a sacred technology for awakening to Presence, to the radiance of our innate state of freedom. Prayer is a sacred technology for dispelling the delusions that cloud our hearts and minds so that we can reside in openheartedness, trust, and caring. Prayer is a sacred technology for bringing us home.

Whatever our institutional affiliation or lack thereof, our relationship to what is holy is in the end a personal affair. We each contact spirit in our own ways, be it through dance, hymns, rosaries, white water, mountain peaks, rose geraniums, talking in tongues, or silence. The path to what is holy is an unfolding and fluid process, created, discovered, invented, and revealed, moment by moment by moment.

Building an Altar

There is a path I walk in the hills near my home that leads through a forest of redwood and oak, madrone and manzanita. About a mile from the trailhead, I pass an old tree with a natural cubbyhole in the foot of its trunk. Hikers lay offerings in the hollow: coins, leaves, flowers, trinkets. One Easter, someone donated a stuffed bunny; at Halloween, a small pumpkin appeared. Each time I take this walk, I linger at the foot of the tree, amused by the mere existence of the spontaneous pilgrimage site. Sometimes I contribute, sometimes not, but always the altar is there, ready and willing to receive whatever passersby choose to give.

In Thailand, altars at the foot of trees are everywhere in the forest, the lower trunks sheathed with bright silk, draped with flower garlands, and the buttressed roots laid with offerings of fruit. Walking along a river in a rainforest in the east of Thailand a few years ago, I was preoccupied with thoughts about my imminent return home when I came across a particularly tall and ancient tree, festooned and decorated. I stopped in my tracks; the great tree indeed deserved my immediate attention. I was grateful for the wisdom of the devotees who, in making the effort to give offerings, reminded me and everyone who passed to stop for a moment and take in the holiness of this banyan. And I realized that in part the function of altars is to attract the attention of the mind and invite us to pay attention to the needs of the soul.

In Nepal, I visited monastery after monastery where monks and nuns adorned altars with flickering butter lamps and rows of brass offering bowls and intricate painted sculptures carved from yak butter. In Latin America, I stepped into dark and cavernous churches where devotees covered altars with votive candles, life-size statues of Jesus and Mary, shining silver medallions of hearts and legs and eyes and elbows and breasts. And on Monday nights I go next door to the zendo where my neighbor lights a stick of incense, touches it to

his forehead, and bows before placing it in a bowl of sand on the altar where
Manjushri, the god of wisdom, sits beside Quan Yin, the goddess of compassion.

Humans build altars—places where we give visual form to the sacred and
address the call of the soul for a home in the material world. And we build
them everywhere: on mantels, windowsills, dashboards, by garden ponds and
at the tops of mountains.

Last week, I received an e-mail that my friend Elaine had passed away. Elaine's
cancer had been metastatic for several years and she had fought it with an un-
quenchable spirit that had mystified her doctors and inspired her friends.
Weeks earlier, I had heard that her kidneys were failing so the news of Elaine's
death did not surprise me, but the loss still cut deep. I turned away from my
work and placed a photograph of Elaine on my altar. She is sitting next to me
on a redwood bench, the ocean behind us, leaning her full head of black curls
against my shoulder. She is wearing red lipstick and smiling straight into the
camera.

Beside the photo, I lit a white candle that would burn for seven days, a
Jewish custom. That night as I lay in bed, the flickering light of the flame crept
through the crack under the bedroom door, and I felt Elaine lingering in my
company even as she departed.

Days after hearing of Elaine's passing, I went to court to deal with a citation I
had found slapped on my windshield after returning to my car from a long
hike. The park police had checked the little box beside "registration expired—
$145." But my registration had not expired, so I checked the little box beside
"not guilty" and mailed the citation to Sacramento, hoping the authorities
would look into the situation, realize their error, and that would be the end of
the matter. Weeks later, I received a form from Sacramento requesting a court
appearance.

I called the judge's clerk and told him there had been a snafu with the DMV's computer. I explained that I had a pile of paperwork to document the fact that the situation had been cleared up, but that I was missing one crucial piece of correspondence. The clerk said, "Oh how awful for you, dear, and I do know things like this happen and I'm so sorry for the inconvenience, but if you come in with the paperwork you *do* have and just tell the truth they're pretty understanding around here, so don't worry about it." His high voice had a cultivated feminine quality and he seemed concerned. "Come an hour early, sign the docket, and you'll be out of here in two hours. They do respect you for making the effort to appear because most people just don't bother to show up. Or you can pay the fine."

Inspired to stand up for justice, I decided to go to court. On the specified date, I woke up at dawn, dressed in my brown suit, put on pearls and lipstick, made my way to the sixteenth floor of the federal building an hour early, signed the docket, and sat down on a pew as the other defendants slowly made their way through the heavy wooden doors. The clerk (who turned out to be a pot-bellied middle-aged man with deep-purple bags under his eyes, indicating a substantial nap might be in order) advised us to confer with one of the students the court had generously provided as counsel, assuring us that although they were not legally qualified to represent us they were smart kids and needed the practice. Mine, an eager young woman with thick calves rising from serious loafers, knitted her dark eyebrows and nodded with sympathy as I related my tale and, agreeing my case was clear-cut, touched my hand for reassurance as she directed me to the set of inner pews.

An hour later, I was called into a back chamber. Two young men with shining complexions presided, apparently honing their barely-out-of-law-school skills. The clerk sat twiddling his pencil, his lips pursed, emitting an air of icy proprietorship. Three police officers in full regalia slouched and chewed gum as they stared off into space, the fluorescent lamps glinting off their polished silver badges. And fifteen other assorted officials whose roles were not divulged stared at me with a dark solemnity. Explaining that my registration had not expired, I pulled out my carefully arranged paper trail which was missing only a single piece of correspondence, and answered the few questions posed by the young men in dark suits who flanked me.

"Please leave the room," the clerk said when I had finished presenting my case. Evidently, the twenty people employed by the state needed to discuss in private this complex criminal situation so they could fully understand the legal nuances. Eons later, I was called back into the chamber and told that further investigation was required. I was given a month to locate the missing piece of correspondence and assured the DMV would cooperate.

"You must be kidding," I said flashing a hard look at the bevy of inquisitors.

"If you prefer," the clerk retorted without a hint of his telephone empathy, "you can take the case to trial."

Was he serious—a judge, a jury? Disbelief dropped my jaw.

"But you assured me I could just tell the truth," I said, flames bursting from my mouth, at which point the clerk asked me to leave the room immediately in a voice that implied handcuffs.

"Presumed guilty until proven innocent," I said as I stuffed my papers into my briefcase. "Blaming the victim," I muttered in the car, stuck in a traffic jam in the parking garage. On the freeway, I whipped into the fast lane and pressed hard on the accelerator. The little Quan Yin sitting on my dashboard altar caught my eye. I slowed down, took a deep breath, and attempted to evoke a molecule of compassion for the employees of the judicial system who were, I told myself, just trying to do their jobs. My anger abated a decibel. Continuing to glance at Quan Yin, I felt a rush of empathy for the victims of injustice throughout the world, and I thought about how incredibly lucky I was, really, and sent waves of compassion out to all people everywhere and promised myself to write a check to Amnesty International.

After a brief interlude at the mall for a bout of shopping therapy during which I purchased a cheer-me-up pair of bright red pants, I arrived home and went straight to the phone to call the DMV. After being on hold for fifteen minutes listening to repeated instructions about which number to press if you wanted recorded instructions about a serious number of further options

(which required further pressing of buttons for more in-depth recorded messages), I managed to talk to a living person who had not a clue about how she
might help. She assured me that no supervisors were available, nor did they
have direct phone lines, but she could take a message.

Dripping tears on the by now dog-eared papers about my car registration,
I put them squarely in the middle of my altar, surrendering the mess to the
great forces of the universe, suggesting the DMV could use some assistance
and I wouldn't mind a teensy bit of help myself. Then I noticed Elaine with her
bright red lipstick and her big wide smile, and she looked right at me with a
friendly but stern kind of stare and winked. Suddenly, I didn't care quite so
passionately about the DMV, and the fine I would most likely end up paying
even though I didn't deserve to, and the fact that justice was not being served.
"Life is a short run, baby," Elaine was whispering in my ear from heaven where
she still had her Mississippi drawl. "Don't be getting yourself all tangled up in
the nonsense. Now lighten up and put on some music and dance."

I picked up the photo and kissed Elaine, my lips covering her whole head
and her bosom. And then I put on music, and I danced. I was not dancing
alone—the clerk and the policemen, the shiny-faced young men, the host of
defendants, legal aides, prosecutors, and Elaine were all dancing with me, my
small living room crowded and swaying.

An altar is a place where we can lay our wounds and our conflicts and our
questions and our scars, giving them to God or to the Great Spirit or to the
little part of our pea brain that is our wisdom lobe and knows what to do but
hasn't kicked in yet. An altar is a place where we lay down our swords and our
shields and we ask for guidance. A visual installation dedicated to whatever we
consider to be holy, an altar is a reminder to the mind to join with the heart.
An altar is personal and mutable and alive, its form and function dictated
solely by the individual who creates it and relates to it: today, a white rose
from the garden; tomorrow, a snapshot of an ailing friend; next week, an audit
letter from the IRS; the next, a pair of dancing shoes.

The Practice

Make an altar, anywhere. On a corner table, a mantel, the top of a filing cabinet, the back of the toilet. Be playful. Be you. Trust your own
aesthetic.

Many altars share common features. A cloth of silk or satin or
white linen representing purification. Candles representing the light of
the divine, the radiance that fills an unencumbered heart. Incense, the
aroma a way to signify through the senses that we are entering sacred
space. Flowers, to signify beauty and the gifts of the natural world.

Some of us are minimalists and our representation of the divine is
made with clean lines: the flower, the candle, the stick of incense
placed in perfect geometry on a polished surface. Others of us are
hopeless holy pack rats and cover our altars in all manner of sacred
finds: brocade, photographs of spiritual teachers in gilded frames, col-
lections of beach glass, a veined stone from a mountain pass, ashes of
pets, sand from the banks of the Ganges, crystals, wands, *dorjes*,
crosses, rattles, rosaries, feathers, leis, bells, wedding bouquets, a
moldy love letter.

I could give you a formula—wash the altar with scented water to
purify the space, choose a color of candle that calls to you, arrange
scented flowers in a vase, add an image of a holy being or a sacred
symbol—but I don't believe in formulas. An altar is too personal a
space for anyone to tell you how to do it. Experiment. Find your own
way. Discover what works for you.

The most important aspect of having an altar is keeping your relationship with it alive. I place all the money that comes my way on the
altar before depositing it in the bank. I put photographs of friends who
are suffering from physical disease or emotional malaise on the altar to
remember them in my heart. I put handwritten wishes on the altar, and
a statue of Quan Yin, who reminds me to be compassionate.

An altar is a space that accepts whatever we offer, that invites our difficulties and fears and hopes and disappointments, that can assist the heart in its movement toward clarity. Change the ritual objects and the way they are arranged as your needs and moods and inclinations shift. Have fun. Make life holy. Life is already holy. We forget and have to remind ourselves.

Invocation

So you've built your altar and there it sits, collecting dust, and that's fine but not as much fun as establishing a living relationship with it. Go ahead and light that candle, refresh the water in the bowls, shower the goddess of love with chocolate sprinkles, chant and pray. But how do we pray, and to whom?

In comparing prayer from a variety of traditions, I have noticed a common, although far from exclusive, architecture of parts: invocation, the expression of gratitude, supplication, and closure. Many rituals begin with a summons—calling upon whatever, whoever, one considers holy and helpful. Invocation turns our minds to Divine Presence, the intelligence and radiance that infuses all being, that is limitless and continues abiding, regardless of our personal birth and death. This quality of limitless, radiant, and intelligent presence resides within our own hearts and so in part what we are invoking when we pray is our own luminous presence. Through prayer, we call upon the wisdom and compassion that exist within us and the universe as an unbroken continuum.

My friend Anna Douglas, a Buddhist teacher at Spirit Rock Meditation Center, told me that when she was ten, she wanted to experience God the way the characters in the Bible did so she prayed fervently every day, reciting the Presbyterian liturgy as it was written, over and over and over again. But she did not have an experience of God the way the characters in the Bible did and she asked to meet with the minister.

"Who wrote the Bible?" Anna asked.

The minister stammered and blushed.

"How do we know it's not just another fairy tale?" she persisted.

The minister had no satisfying answer, and Anna, deciding the Bible was fiction, ceased praying.

Years later, as a young actress, Anna was cast to play Joan of Arc in a summer-stock production. She had been trained in Method acting and to prepare for her role, Anna fully immersed herself in the character. Every day of the rehearsal period, she walked through the woods for hours, praying ceaselessly, the way she imagined Joan of Arc had prayed. This time, she told me, she found God.

"And what was God?" I asked. "Or who?"

"God was all of being," Anna said without even a moment of hesitation. "Radiant, undifferentiated, luminous being—the trees, the sky, the sun, the birds, the song of the birds, the rocks, the clouds, the grasses. God was everywhere, inside of me and outside of me and I became very happy and God was happiness."

———

One way to begin our prayers is to call upon whatever qualities or deities or goddesses or God we have an affinity with or a need for and to acknowledge their presence, here, now. *Blessed is God.* If we are confused and caught in delusion, we can call upon the wisdom aspect of the Divine to be present, to be felt, to come alive within our own hearts. *God of Clarity and Wisdom, may I be free of obfuscation, may I see deeply, may I reach understanding.* If we are angry, we can call upon the compassionate aspect of the divine, to be felt, alive within our own hearts. *Goddess of Compassion, may I feel with your heart. May my own heart soften with the light of wisdom and loving-kindness.* If we, or our friends, are in need of healing, we can call upon the healing aspect of the Divine to be present, to do her work in our own body or the body of a friend. *God of Healing, may you bring balance into this body, into this mind.*

We can invoke the spirits of water and fire and air and earth to nourish us and guide us and accompany us. We can call out to the spirit of the eagle and the whale and the daddy longlegs and the deer, each unique with intelligence and capacities that can assist us in wisdom and action. We can call out to our ancestors and our teachers.

The holy books say that God has ten thousand names and will answer to any of them. But we do not need to open a holy book to discover the names of God—they are written in the landscape and etched into the beating of our own hearts.

The Practice

Whenever you feel the need or inclination, call upon whomever you want to be present in the inner and outer realms. You can pray in a formal way, lighting a candle and incense on your altar, reciting a mantra or prayer you have learned, or you can make up your own words. You can call on Divine Presence, God, Jesus, Mary, Allah, Hashem, Padmasambhava, Tara, the Dakas and Dakinis, saying their names, chanting their names.

Experiment with praying anywhere when the inclination arises. While you are walking in the woods, you can invoke the spirit of the trees and creeks and flowers and grasses, the sun and the sky, the critters, greeting them or asking for their help. *Spirit of the Oak Tree, Spirit of the Clouds, Spirit of the Falling Leaves, walk with me.* While you are driving, you can call on the spirit of safety and well-being. *May I be protected. May I be safe.* While you are taking a bath or showering, you can call on the spirit of water for purification. *May you wash away my confusion. May you wash away my fear. May my body and heart be purified.* While you are gardening, you can call on the spirit of the earth and the sun and moon, and the spirit of the plants, to help the garden grow. *May the corn be sweet and tall, the radishes plump and pungent.*

You can pray for your own well-being and for the well-being of others, sending wishes for the happiness of all beings out into the universe on blessing waves.

Make up your own words, your own melodies, or improvise with ones you have learned that move you. Or make up wordless prayers. Oooommmmmm.

Gratitude

In the afternoons, my grandmother sat in her mission-style rocking chair, a green blanket she had crocheted when her hands were still nimble laid over her knees, and at unpredictable moments she burst into prayer.

"Hallelujah, hallelujah," she began and, free of any restraint, rasped out Hebrew prayers in her trembling voice.

One afternoon, I asked her to teach me a prayer that I had heard her sing for many years. We sat together at her dining room table, her knobby fingers shaking as she pointed to the words in the prayer book, and went over the melody and pronunciation line by line until I, too, knew it by heart. "All the trees and all the grasses are singing praises," she translated.

After that, each time she broke into the prayer, I joined her. Bolstered by the duet, she went on with her second-favorite prayer, "O beautiful, for spacious skies . . ."

My grandma chanted blessings of grace before eating each meal, and a blessing of grace after she had taken her last bite and laid her fork down. She chanted blessings in the morning when she woke up and at night before she slept. At the end of each visit when I hugged her good-bye, my coat buttoned and purse in hand, she blessed me in Hebrew, a whispered prayer that came strong from her heart even when she was so ancient she could barely keep track of the days, her wishes for my well-being gaining power as her physical vitality diminished.

I worried that when my grandmother died the prayers would fade from my life like old photographs, the words and meanings of the liturgy disappearing until finally the pages of memory would be blank. To keep the prayers alive, I needed not only to learn them, but also to recite them. I started with a Hebrew prayer I had been fond of since childhood, the *shehechiyanu:* "Blessed be the Creator for having sustained us, kept us, given us life so that we are here at this moment." The prayer traditionally is chanted on the festivals, and when we have the pleasure to taste the first food of a season, when a child is born, or when the first flower of spring emerges from bud. We say it anytime we feel inspired to give gratitude for being alive, able to celebrate that moment's offering. How grateful we are to be here, now. I chant the prayer the way I imagine a cantor would, loud and heartfelt, opening my mouth wide: "Blessed is the Creator, for granting us life, for sustaining us, and keeping us, until this moment. Amen."

The expression of gratitude, or even just the feeling of gratitude, is the heart of prayer, says Brother David Steindl-Rast. When we look around and pay attention, we perceive that our lives are given to us freely; that the air we breathe, and the water that falls from the sky and quenches our thirst, and the sun that rises and sheds light, and the trees that give us shelter, and the food that grows from the earth are all given freely. The beauty of this world and our ability to perceive it are given freely. We are sustained moment to moment to moment, day in and day out until our last breath, by uncountable gifts.

Despite this abundance, we often feel deprived, as if we do not have enough, as if we, ourselves, are inherently insufficient, and so we suffer. When we learn to turn our minds to the gifts we are provided—the miracle of carrot tufts poking their way through the dark earth, of purple plums frosted with plum breath, of lilacs, of sea foam, of the melody of red-winged blackbirds, and the miracle of our having been born at all, with senses to receive this wonder—when we turn our minds to perceive what is given, gratitude awakens within us, and we fall in love with this life and this moment. This love, always available whenever we turn our gaze in its direction, is what is called freedom; this love is what is called God.

The Practice

At some time during the day, take a moment to appreciate right then whatever is provided. This practice takes no time at all, only attention. Drinking a swig from your water bottle, appreciate water. Talking with a friend, appreciate companionship. Eating a bite of Caesar salad, appreciate anchovies and croutons and Parmesan and hearts of romaine and taste buds. Riding in the subway, appreciate the mass of humanity, everyone unique, everyone mortal. Dedicate a moment, each day, to appreciation. To gratitude.

You can appreciate silently the panoply of gifts each moment provides, or you can say the words out loud: "This living body still breathing; my cocker spaniel, Emma, with long ears that flop when she bounds; the cool wind coming through a crack in the window and touching my bare arms; the view of a cove of beach from my studio window; what luck, a sunny day and time enough to take a walk, to breathe the sea-salt air. Thank you, God of Gifts, for such fine offerings."

Supplication

When diagnosed with an ambiguous and potentially life-threatening disease a couple of years ago, I confided in the woman who cleans my house that I was undergoing a health crisis. She told me to pray. "But you cannot just whisper your prayers," she said, "you have to clamor."

Julia told me that when her son had been ill, she awoke each night at 2 A.M., kneeled on the floor, and clamored. Her son had been healed. She told me that when a friend was diagnosed with cancer, she again awoke in the middle of the night and for weeks, fell to her knees, and clamored. Her friend, too, had been healed.

While I did not find myself clamoring in the night on my knees, I did appreciate Julia's advice. We can pray with ardor, with passion, with rigor, with strong intent, rather than praying with half a heart, our voices laced with cynicism, our minds quick with doubt. And if we do so, whether or not our prayers are answered in the way we desire, we will have experienced freedom while praying—the freedom of true expression, the freedom of an outpouring heart—and that freedom is in itself an answer to our prayers.

Most of us come to a point in our lives, once in a lifetime, or once a year, or once a week, or sixteen times a day, when we feel the need for spiritual assistance. Perhaps we are grief-stricken from the death of a loved one, or our child becomes ill, or the market crashes days after we've invested our nest egg. Perhaps we are phobic about flying, or madly obsessed with an unrequited romance, or addicted to some intoxicating substance, or have been trying on bathing suits in a dressing room with three-way mirrors, or all of the above. At some point or another, most of us want guidance, assistance, comfort, and healing.

At times like these, one option is to burst into fearless prayer. But most of us are afraid to burst into even mumbled-under-the-breath prayer and unsure of how to even begin such utterances. All that is necessary to become skillful at prayer is to practice praying, and within moments we discover the act is utterly familiar.

One way to ask for assistance is to do just that; belt out, "Help! Help! Help!" We can sing like Aretha Franklin, "H-E-L-P, Help." Or Pavoratti, "Heeelllllp! Heeellllllp!" Frank Sinatra, "Help, shoo be do be, Help, shoo be do be." Or the Beatles, "Won't you please, please help me." Help might come in the instant movement of traffic which was at a dead halt, or in the interior movement of the heart, which now that it is singing, feels uplifted even if the traffic is as still as roadkill.

Years ago, I attended a Rosh Hashanah service in Villeneuve, a suburb of Paris populated by Algerian Jews. I sat in the balcony with the other women, shielded behind a lace curtain. Below us, bearded men in black suits and stiff hats rocked back and forth, chanting. The rabbi stood in the middle of the dark and moving sea, intoning the new year's sermon like a Baptist preacher, mellifluous and commanding:

> *"We do not ask for wealth or health*
> *for ourselves and our family on Rosh Hashanah,*
> *We ask for peace for the world,*
> *for the soul to be at peace,*
> *We ask for the soul to be united with God.*
> *When our spiritual needs are met,*
> *all else will follow.*
> *If the soul is not at peace,*
> *nothing will follow.*
> *When all we seek are material things,*
> *we will get nothing.*
> *When we ask for love,*
> *for peace in the soul,*
> *then true health,*
> *then true wealth will follow."*

The most profound prayer is the quest of the heart to find the path to peace. The awakened heart is at ease with whatever unfolds moment to moment. When the heart is resting in equanimity, the body is most likely to achieve a state of health and the mind most able to discover solutions to what appear to be insoluble conflicts. When we pray for material things, the rabbi said, we will receive nothing. When we pray for peace, we will be given all.

The Practice

The next time you are feeling in need of assistance and your family and friends aren't sufficient to the task at hand, call out for help. You can ask for specific help for a particular need, or for the heart to be at peace and the mind at ease. You can sing or chant or wail or whisper. You can address someone in particular: God, Jesus, Tara, Allah, Hashem. Or the universe at large. Try it. Experiment. Clamor.

The Poetry of Seeing

One of the common beliefs about prayer is that the desired outcome is most likely to occur if we see it clearly in our mind's eye. Prayer, then, need not be a supplication directed to a being outside of ourselves, but a visualization of our wishes.

When dealing with my health crisis, precancerous cells that posed no immediate threat but had the potential to develop into a more dangerous condition, I did a complementary treatment, a plant extract that was administered intravenously. A nurse came to my house to set up my IV and then left me alone for three hours as the medication entered my veins one yellow droplet at a time. Instead of watching television or reading to distract myself, I worked with the imagery tapes made available by Dr. Martin Rossman. For one of the guided sessions, you allow an image of healing to arise in the mind. I saw perfectly circular cells that were made of light and filled all the parts of my body. As I sat for hours bathed in light, I became happier and happier, and rather than dreading the biweekly treatments, I began to look forward to them.

My friends asked me with concerned looks how I was doing. Despite the fact that I enjoy complaining more than almost any other verbal activity, I found myself admitting that I was doing quite well, thank you; because, in fact, after weeks of imagining every single cell of my body radiating light, I felt aglow. "You do look good," my friends acknowledged, wondering if I had changed my hairdo or lost some weight or something. "Light," I said.

The doctors, unaccustomed to light cures and esoteric plant extracts, incorrectly assessed that my alternative therapies were not working and prevailed upon me to have surgery. After months of resisting their advice, I finally succumbed. Again, I turned for assistance to the work of Dr. Rossman. To aid in the ease of surgical procedures and postsurgical healing, he suggests the patient visualize him or herself fully recovered and engaged in a favorite activity that is representative of complete well-being. As the nurses in their pastel shower caps and matching booties fastened the gurney straps and wheeled me down the shining hospital corridors and through the swinging doors of the operating room, I imagined myself dancing like Isadora Duncan—pirouetting and leaping, my legs extended in grand arabesques, a frothy skirt billowing around my knees.

Only weeks after my surgery, I performed at a conference held not far from my home. As I danced across the stage in a lavender skirt that billowed as I spun, I realized I was living the vision I had seen in my mind's eye. I knew in my bones that the visualization a month earlier had contributed to making the vision a reality and while I may never fully understand the mechanisms of this process, I will never cease to feel grateful for the effects.

In order to communicate with the subconscious and the autonomic nervous system, which is in part where healing occurs, we use symbolic language. If we imagine ourselves fully well and engaged in an activity that is symbolic of total healing, we are more likely to experience that outcome than if we imagine the worst possible events that might occur if the disease progresses or surgery fails or secondary effects manifest. If we imagine ourselves doing what we love to do, we are more likely to find ourselves engaged in that very activity.

The Papago, a Native American tribe living in the desert of Arizona, take this process a step further, singing their prayers to invoke particular ends. "The describing of a desired event in the magic of beautiful speech was to them the means by which to make that event take place," writes Ruth Underhill in her wonderful book *Singing for Power*. "The songs are from every department of life and in many moods: solemn, wistful, humorous, wild. The mood does not matter. Magic will be worked if the description is vivid and if the singing or the recitation is done, as it should be . . . on behalf of all the people."

The Practice

When you have a strong desire for your own or others' well-being, practice visualization. See in your mind's eye whatever it is that you wish for, but instead of visualizing only material things—a new car, a winning lottery ticket—move more deeply into the needs of the heart. If you are ill or depressed, imagine yourself engaged in an activity that represents complete well-being, an activity you love, and see the scene in vivid detail.

If a friend is ill, see the friend as radiant. If you are planting, you might imagine the garden abloom and fruitful. If you are getting married, you might imagine the light of love infusing all the guests and participants. If you are starting a new job, you might imagine you and your boss and fellow employees moving in harmonious patterns together.

Make up a melody and sing the prayer, describing the image "in the magic of beautiful speech."

I am riding on the back
of an Appaloosa mare
and she is running, running,
her mane dark against her neck,

and she is running, running,
over a field of wild grasses
and her flank is wet with heat
and she is running.

Have fun, play with words and melody, rhythm and repetition.
You can pray for your own needs, for the needs of a friend, for
peace in the world, for the protection of the planet.

And Then We Say, "Amen"

The last time I saw my father was on a Friday night when I dropped by his Menlo Park condominium for dinner on my way home from teaching in Big Sur. His wife was away for the weekend, so Pops had cooked the meal himself—pasta tubes with tomato sauce and mushrooms, a salad with avocado, and bread with peppered dipping oil. My nineteen-year-old nephew, Jonathon, a sophomore majoring in mathematics at Stanford, was visiting as well. We set a table on the patio overlooking the vast green of a golf course and sat in the dim light of evening. Pleased to have an audience, my father gushed with stories and unsolicited advice.

"Jonathon, you need a haircut," he said as he rolled an olive pit out of his mouth and frowned at my nephew's bleached dreadlocks.

"He looks great," I insisted, admiring the chaos of tufts.

"Yech," my father said, offering me more salad. His own hair was silver at the temples and his pate was going bald.

Jonathon, who opts for silence at moments like this, said nothing, but I detected the hint of a grin.

As I hugged my father goodbye, I said if he was tired, I could drive Jonathon down the hill to his dorm. The curve of my father's back had deepened with age and I imagined he suffered considerable pain although he rarely complained. He said no, no, he was happy to make the drive, and I saw a quick glance pass between the two men and suspected the grandfather and grandson would enjoy each other's company alone in the car, talking about equations.

Late on Sunday night, my telephone rang. I was surprised to hear my half-sister's voice. "Are you all right?" I asked. "No," she said in a near whisper, "Daddy is dead."

I was not able to take in the meaning of her words although I knew what each word meant. He had been out to dinner with his wife and another couple. He had stepped outside for some air and collapsed. By the time the ambulance arrived, his heart could not be revived.

Two friends were visiting from Los Angeles and we had just finished dinner. "My father died," I whispered. My voice sounded calm coming out of my lips, which were miles away from the place where I had formulated the words. Then I rolled onto the floor and watched from a distant place of intimate calm: *She is weeping, she is on the floor, her face is wet, her father is dead, this is grief, this woman wailing, me.*

Even though my father appeared to be in good health for a man of his age, and his thinking revealed not a jot of cell damage, I had been expecting this call for years, dreading it, anxious whenever the phone rang late at night that he had been struck down. And now the moment had come—and gone—the waiting was over, the call received, the phone returned to its holder. Already my friends spoke about my father in the past tense. He was, they said, a charming and a complicated man.

For years, I had spoken to Pops nearly every week. I visited him frequently and confided in him the moment I encountered success or difficulty. I could imagine him lying on the sidewalk outside of the restaurant, the diners still conversing over sea bass and sirloin, but I could not imagine him lifeless. He was too vital a man, too fatherly, to be gone.

Two days later at the funeral, the rabbi handed us black ribbons. It is a Jewish custom to rip one's clothing as a symbol of grief, but these days you save your clothing and tear the ribbon. The rabbi instructed us to pin the ribbon over our hearts and asked us to repeat after him, *"Baruch dayan ha'emet."*

Blessed be the true judge. I repeated the prayer, *"Baruch dayan ha'emet."* Blessed be the true judge. The time of my father's birth and death were out of my hands. All I could do was surrender to God's way.

Weeks have passed, but still my chest tightens and tears squeeze out of my eyes and my nose gets snivelly. One moment, in the middle of scrubbing the crust from a burnt frying pan, I am overcome with fury; the next moment, when I am in the garden, a pang of loss sharp as a surgeon's scalpel arises with the sweet aroma of basil leaves. And when I sit down with my bowl of oatmeal, disappointment rages that he departed without a whisper of warning when we still had so much left to talk about. My wise friends say yes, the emotions that follow death are complex.

For the days and nights immediately following his death, I move in slow motion from the couch, to the easy chair, to the bed. Most days I imagine picking up the phone and calling him, "Pops, it's Nina." Imagine him saying, "Ninkela," a happiness in his voice. "Ninkela," the sound of two crystal glasses touching.

And then there are moments of grace when I drift into the welcome release of a sensed perfection: my father, an aged man, passed swiftly and without pain, fresh from a trip to Provence where the mustard fields painted the landscape a stunning yellow and the turquoise Mediterranean stretched to the horizon. My father, a sailor, loved the sea. Blessed be the true judge.

⁓⁓⁓⁓⁓

Weeks after my father's death, I attended a meditation retreat with the Tibetan lama, Tsoknyi Rimpoche. During the seven days of silence, Tsoknyi taught us to meditate in an open way, allowing all thoughts and feelings to arise and pass away in the big sky of consciousness. When I had done this practice before under his guidance, I experienced a great spaciousness of being and found myself quite content. This time, however, a big strong grief arose and would not dissipate despite my efforts to recognize its essential nature as pure light, pure emptiness. Toward the end of the retreat, I confessed my difficulties to Rimpoche.

"You do not turn grief into light," he said. "You grieve."

Rimpoche explained that a bodhisattva is a being who upon becoming enlightened vows to always embody in human form and dedicates his or her life to altruistic action in an effort to alleviate the suffering of all beings. This I had heard. But he continued to explain that "sattva" means courage. Becoming a bodhisattva does not mean that you do not suffer, he said. Becoming a bodhisattva means you become a warrior and are willing to feel deeply the suffering that is a part of human life. As you build your courage and open yourself more and more to feeling this pain, then you develop true compassion. And as compassion arises, the pain is no longer suffering; the pain is also joy because the heart is broken open.

In Judaism there is a saying: "A broken heart is the gateway to heaven."

The Buddhists recite the three awarenesses: "We are aware that we cannot avoid losing the ones that we love. We are aware that we cannot avoid disease and decay. We are aware that we cannot avoid old age and dying." Everyone we love will one day die. We ourselves will one day become sick and pass away. This is the Dharma, the Tao, the way of this world into which we are born. But most of us do not keep death on our left shoulder, as the Yaqui shaman Don Juan advised, to remind us that this life flies by in an instant.

Regardless of how often we forget or what we wish were true, this life does fly by in an instant. And in the stretch of that instant, we are given the opportunity to celebrate—to love fully, to live fully, to express fully the joys and the sorrows of the heart. If we accept this mission of living fully, it is incumbent upon us to dance on beaches and prairies and mountaintops, to sing in forests and backyards and city streets, and to make art in the nooks and crannies of this planet earth where we have found ourselves alive together. We have also been given the task by the great powers that be to let go, over and over again, to surrender to God's will, to the Tao, to the Way Life Is. And as we surrender and behold this universe of infinite and fleeting creation, we will resound with a grand hallelujah. And then we will say, "Amen."

How do we close our prayers? We say, "May my prayers and actions be of benefit to all beings." We say, "So be it." We say, "Let it be." We say, "Thy will be
done, thy will not mine." We say, "Svaha." We say, "Blessed be the true judge."
We say, "Amen." We put our hands together and bow. We touch our forehead
to the ground.

ten

Bringing
Art
to Life

Improvisational Being

"Through spontaneity we are re-formed into ourselves. It creates
an explosion that for the moment frees us from handed-down
frames of reference, memory choked with old facts and
information and undigested theories and techniques of other
people's findings. Spontaneity is the moment of personal freedom when we are faced with a reality and see it, explore it and
act accordingly. In this reality the bits and pieces of ourselves
function as an organic whole. It is the time of discovery, of
experiencing, of creative expression."
—VIOLA SPOLIN

Living Art

According to me and most of my friends in the art world, Linda Montano is the reigning queen of integrating life and art. For example, the first winter after marrying her photographer husband, she was preparing to visit her in-laws in Florida. Uneasy about whether or not her wardrobe was suitable for an extended stay with Mitchell's classy parents, she did not fret alone, rifling through her closet, trying on outfit after outfit in front of a full-length mirror, and discarding all options as she wondered how she had ever thought any of them remotely attractive. No. Linda called her friends and staged a fashion show in her living room where she paraded up and down a ramp in her bathing suit and towel, her sundress and spectacles, her shorts, her slacks, her pajamas. Mitchell took photographs and the audience voiced their approval or disapproval; and later, Linda packed her suitcase with the confidence engendered by community taste.

I was lucky to spend time with Linda. She was a mad and brilliant playmate, and I learned from her that it is possible to transform life into art. Making dinner became an opera of arias about chopping onions and sauteeing green beans. Clothing became costume. Park lawns became dance halls. Strangers became angels who bestowed savvy bits of sage advice. We were not interested in the making of an object to frame and sell, but in the making of rich and meaningful lives. And we were convinced that meaning resided not in things but in the way we lived.

Making life art requires that we create our lives, moment to moment—and life presents us with abundant opportunities for prayer and play and celebration and self-expression. No one can make our lives holy except ourselves: no guru, no priest, no abbot, no preacher, no minister, no sadhu, no astrologer, no therapist, no channel, no rabbi, no lover, no parent, no child, no friend. But everyone can help.

Play Date

The morning after my father's funeral, my brother flew off to the Mayo Clinic to have open-heart surgery. He had scheduled the operation months before, and the danger of postponing the valve repair outweighed the emotional discomfort of proceeding during this time of shock and grief. My brother was resolute and relatively calm, at least as far as I could assess from our phone conversations. I, however, was in total meltdown, afraid that my brother would follow my father into the great embrace of the painless beyond. So I called my friend Kat and told her I needed her help—could I spend the night before my brother's surgery, and could we do a healing ceremony together? Kat is an ethnobotanist who has been conducting fieldwork with the Indians of southern Mexico for years and has a deep respect for tribal wisdom and spiritual technology. And I've known her since I was a teenager so I'm not worried about falling apart in her company.

Kat built an altar, lit a bundle of sage, and we wafted the smoke over each other's bodies with a fan of feathers. We sat facing one another in the dark, shaking our rattles, two grown-up women who had met on their first day of college and now colored their hair to hide the gray, sitting cross-legged on the floor and calling on the spirits of healing. Kat prayed that my brother be protected through his surgery, that his heart be repaired so that he could continue to do his work as a doctor and heal his own patients, that his life be long so that he could continue to parent his children into adulthood, that his heart be healed from grief and sadness. I shook the rattle and prayed that the surgeon's hands be intelligent and kind. That the pain be minimal. That there be no complications. That my brother's heart find a regular beat again and carry him through this life as my companion and friend. Kat prayed and I prayed and Kat prayed and I prayed, letting our hearts speak through our lips to his heart. We prayed until we had no words left and I finally felt calm.

I could have prayed alone, but I didn't want to; I wanted company and support and intimacy.

I met Paul at Esalen after I had given a performance. He approached me and told me he thought I was brilliant, so I immediately liked him. We couldn't settle into a lengthy discussion however, because moments before, while the applause was still lingering in the air, I had slid a CD into the deck and turned up the bass and now the room was rollicking with dancing bodies. Paul (whose name I did not know at the time) gave up any attempt at conversation and dissolved into the crowd of dancers.

When the dancing ended, however, we did speak for a moment, and the conversation has continued, off and on, to this day. A French writer, Paul was researching an article about the New Age capitals of America. Over the course of the next few months, our traveling schedules coincided and we met in Santa Fe and Manhattan and continued the conversation we had initiated in Big Sur, which had four consistent themes: art, work, love, and enlightenment. But the conversation did not unfold through language alone.

When I visited Paul at his hotel on Manhattan's Upper East Side, we hadn't seen each other for months. As he opened the door, he gestured to two chairs he had placed facing a window. We had both learned a meditation practice called sky gazing (which I describe later in this book), and without speaking, we sat down and stared out the window for half an hour, allowing our minds to soften into the spaciousness of the vast sky, despite the fact that the view was obstructed by an adjacent high-rise and all we could see of the blue was a slit at the very top of the window. Then we went on a wander through Central Park, during which Paul carried on in an American accent and I in a French accent, playfully trading components of our identities, he being French and I, American. We ended up in front of the glass-walled aquarium in Central Park where penguins, propelling themselves from under the water by a sudden flexing of their feet, shot upward and landed standing upright on the bank, looking as if they had never been in the water at all. At this point Paul and I reverted to our normal dialects.

We met in Santa Fe where I took up residence in a small casita to write, and Paul had sessions with past-life regressionists and entity-channeling psychics. In the evenings, as the sun set on the flat desert horizon, we sat sky gazing on my front porch until all the fingers of blazing color had faded. Next, we put on music and danced hard on the Mexican tiles. One night, realizing the full moon was aglow on acres of cacti, we carried our cane-back chairs into the yard and chanted "Ram, Ram, Ram" at the alabaster disc, making up melodies and harmonies even though neither of us had much of a relationship with Ram.

Whenever and wherever we have met during the past few years, we have meditated, danced, chanted, and read to each other from our own and other's writing. We have not crawled into bed together; we are not lovers. Instead, we have invented a friendship.

There are many ways to spend time with our friends, and if we are courageous, we will call upon one another to meet on the playing field and devote our time together to the highest end, which is not an end, but the freedom of expression with which each of us is gifted at birth.

The Practice

Make a date with a friend and write it down in ink on your calendar. Decide together on a way of spending time that is inventive and artful and playful and that meets your needs of the moment. You might devote some of the time to meditating and chanting. You might devote some of the time to dancing. You might devote some of the time to singing. You might devote some of the time to drawing or painting or sculpting. You might decide to spend some of the time writing. You might decide to dress up and go out on the town in character. You might decide to give each other foot massages and do rituals with incantations and brews and flower petals. You might decide to make soup for a friend who is sick or make jam from the fruit growing in your yard or decorate a cake. You might decide to paint furniture or arrange flowers. Or clean out the garage while you sing. Or design a garden. You might decide to take a picnic to the beach and build sculptures in the sand.

Do what you enjoy doing and do what you have never done before. Walk backward clapping your hands. Make a set in the backyard with candles and branches and read poetry to each other.

Do not go out to dinner and to a movie.

Do not watch television.

Do not rent a video.

Make your own movie.

Ten Practices for the Art of Daily Life

Most likely, you can invent your own activities, but for those times when you're feeling fog-brained and weak-kneed and want someone else to take you by the hand and say, "Here, do this," the way your mother used to do when you were a kid and you didn't have to figure everything out by yourself, I offer these suggestions:

1. WRAPPING PAPER ART AND THE LIKE

Instead of buying wrapping paper, greeting cards, postcards, make your own.

For gift wrap, pull out old newspaper, used paper bags, butcher paper, or big newsprint pads, and a handful of colored pens, rubber stamps, and crayons. Make designs. These need not be elaborate or perfect or resemble anything you might find in a store or the pages of glossy homemaker magazines. Just have fun. Make swirls and polka dots, splatter paint, draw hearts and daisies. Whatever. Don't worry. Be happy.

Save old calendars and use them to wrap gifts (I heard that the Japanese did this because paper was so scarce and, never knowing myself what to do with beautiful calendars at the end of the year, I took up the practice and it works amazingly well—very arty and elegant).

Pick flowers from the garden to decorate packages (roses, daisies, pansies) or use colored rubber bands.

When you are on vacation, make your own postcards, illustrating your impressions of foreign lands. Art stores carry pads of blank postcards, or you can make your own on paper you find while you travel.

You can make seasonal cards (Christmas, Valentine's Day) with your friends and your kids and your kid friends. Pull out art supplies (scissors, glue sticks, crayons, paper, pens, paints, brushes, feathers, shells, yarn, fabric, rubber stamps, stencils) and spend an afternoon or an evening making art cards. People enjoy making art together so it is an act of generosity to provide them the opportunity.

You can also do this alone—when you want to send a love note or a get-well wish or a thank-you card. You can take time, or do this very quickly, taking only a few seconds to draw on an envelope before you send it, or seal it with a kiss. The recipient will be grateful.

2. WALL PRAYERS

When you are painting a room, before rolling on the first coat, write prayers on the walls. You can write them with a pencil or a paintbrush. You can pray for love and passion in the bedroom, joviality and friendship in the dining room, equanimity in the living room, purification in the bathroom, success for the benefit of all beings in the office. You can pray for good tastes and radiant health in the kitchen, for peace and happiness everywhere. You can invoke the names of gods and goddesses. The prayers will be covered by paint and invisible to the eye, but will reside in the walls of the room as hidden treasures radiating blessings.

3. FOOD ART

Imagine the dinner plate is a blank canvas and create a design, a painting, a sculpture with food. Pay attention to color and shape, texture and pattern. You can make the kind of design you see in fine restaurants or the pages of *Gourmet* magazine, or you can make up your own style of painting with food. Landscapes—a flat bed of rice with asparagus standing upright is a forest. Portraits—a goat-cheese woman with eyes made of almonds, lashes and eyebrows of pine nuts, a smile of pumpkin seeds, parsley hair. Play with pattern—drizzle olive oil in curlicues, make a checkerboard of cheddar and Swiss cheese with carrot and beet medallions as the checkers, design a mandala of multicolored cherry tomatoes and olives. Get the kids to help, or the dinner guests. People like making art with food.

4. BATHTUB POETRY

Read poetry out loud to yourself as you lie in a bubble bath in candlelight. If you happen to speak another language (even only a few words), find a book of poetry in that tongue (with translations). You will feel as though you are in another country, another time, as though you are someone else. Trust me on this one. It's really fun. Do it.

5. RARE FOOD

When you're shopping at the grocery store or the local farmers market, find something you don't usually eat, buy it, take it home, and taste.

Humans like habits. We prefer to go to the movie theater we always go to, to wake up at a certain time of day, to eat particular foods. While some habits can be healthful, like exercising regularly and meditating, others can limit us from living fully. By breaking a single habit, we can expand our range of experience. By eating a food we don't normally eat, we can awaken all of our senses.

Before eating your chosen food—the caviar, or chermoya, the red banana, the seaweed salad, the green tea ice cream, or the tricolor corn—take a
few moments to simply look at it. Notice its shape, color, the patterns on its
surface. Smell the fragrance of the food. Finally, take a bite, and notice the flavor, the texture, the complexity of tastes. You might hate how the food tastes,
or love it and want to race back to the market for more. No matter. Either
way you are expanding your palate and your knowledge of the world.

You do not have to go to Bhutan or the heart of the Amazon to experience
the world as exotic. You can break a simple habit of behavior, for an instant,
and taste the unusual with all of your attention.

6 .   C U T   U P S

Reach into your paper recycling bin, grab a piece at random and cut or tear it
up into small pieces (less than one square inch each). Select five or six of the
pieces that contain phrases you find of interest and build a sequence, a poem.
Give yourself one minute.

I took a one-minute break just now to do this practice:

> *to cross her lips*
> *an honorable*
> *at a time and*
> *the whole day ahead*
> *harder*
> *cut through*
> *dark forest*

The mind locks into a linear way of thinking which is not necessarily a creative
way of thinking. Working with random language and images, we can free the
mind from its tight grip on linearity. When you go back to whatever you were
doing, writing a report or doing the bookkeeping, you might notice that your
mood has shifted, that you feel more lighthearted.

If you are in the midst of a difficult problem, take a one-minute break to do this practice. When the mind frees itself from a stressful problem, even for a moment, one's whole being can feel refreshed, and when you return to the challenge at hand, you might proceed with more clarity.

7.   ITEM   EXCHANGE

When you give a dinner party, invite your guests to remove something they are wearing—a sock, a necklace, a tie, a hat, a scarf—and put it on the person sitting to their right.

What we wear has great importance to us. We might love red socks, or have an emotional attachment to a necklace given to us by a grandmother. We might put on a hat to lift our spirits when we're feeling dull. Clothing also carries gender implications: men don't wear pearl necklaces; women don't wear neckties. When we exchange a part of what we claim as our identity, and take on a part of someone else's, an inner loosening can occur. A man who would never be seen without his tie is suddenly tie-less and wearing a woman's hat. A woman who only wears understated jewelry is up to her elbow in bangles. A simple exchange of an item can transform an entire personality. Be open to what happens. Let characters emerge. And remember to have everyone reclaim their things before going home—unless they are ready to give them up for good.

8.   THE   ART   OF   THE   PHONE   MESSAGE

Make up a ditty for your answering machine message. I mean, let's face it, we do not enjoy being told uncountable times that "no one can come to the phone right now so please leave a message after the beep." Still, we have to leave messages for our friends and family, so this is a perfect opportunity to "be creative." Talk in an accent. Record the sound of your backyard at dawn or your teakettle boiling or the street you live on or your cat meowing or your kid tap dancing. I had a series of messages of sounds that appeared to be other than what they were: *this is the sound of a vitamin jar masquerading as a maraca: this is the sound of the faucet pretending to be a rainforest waterfall.*

Tell some quirky story about your day. Relate trivia that you find fascinating. I learned this evening that in order to cling to ceilings and walls, geckos emit static electricity through their feet—and then, when they want to move, they turn the electricity off. Cool.

9. FURNITURE DANCING

Dance in bed, enjoying the softness of the mattress. Roll, tumble, fall. Dance about on the couch, letting your knees hang over the rolled arms, or the back. Zip around on your rolling ergonomic desk chair, waving your arms, extending your legs after pushing off. Spin. Hang from the doorjamb lengthening your spine, stretching your arms. Slide down the banister.

10. THE GREAT OUTDOORS

Roll down a grassy hill or a sand dune. Skip across a park lawn. Run as fast as you can. Jump.

Yes/And

You have a craving for baked chicken the way your grandma used to cook it, so you go to the store in the middle of the afternoon, buy a chicken and potatoes and carrots, and pull out the file card with your grandmother's recipe. An hour later, your husband calls, says he's had a hankering for Chinese food, do you want to meet him at the restaurant downtown with the pink tablecloths? Most likely, you say no, automatically. But maybe there is a way that your husband's craving for Chinese food and yours for baked chicken can both be incorporated into the same evening.

In the world of improvisation, we call the skill of incorporating divergent realities yes/and. This means that when a partner offers you an image for a scene, you are obligated to accept it even if the scene differs dramatically from the one you had in mind. For instance, two actors, Robert and Nancy, might begin moving their arms vigorously at their sides. Robert imagines he is in a canoe on a lake at dawn and says, "The water is glassy, the clouds are pink in the morning sky and the red-winged blackbirds are singing." Nancy, who is moving her arms in exactly the same fashion as Robert, has imagined they are at the gym after work. Her impulse is to say, "No, we are not on a lake, you toad, we're at the 24 Hour Nautilus in the mall." Instead, Nancy checks her impulse and accepts Robert's offer without abandoning her own image. "I'm glad we've been working out at the 24 Hour Nautilus every evening," she says, "because I feel like I could row until dusk."

As I work with my performance partners, I am startled at how often the impulse to refuse an offer emerges, at how I must repeatedly and instantaneously recognize and dispel the urge and instead find an inventive way of incorporation—of saying yes, what you are seeing is valid and what I am seeing is valid and somehow they can fit together into one story.

So how do we apply this to real life? Often when we communicate with a friend or partner, we polarize, taking opposing stances when in fact our positions are less fixed than the arguments we are espousing. By working to accept one another's sentiments, we open our minds to experiencing reality in a more complex light. Keeping the mind porous is not easy; incorporation requires that we stretch ourselves and expand our sense of what is possible. As we make room for each other's sentiments we find ourselves more able to admit the paradoxes that live within our own hearts. As we learn to embrace our partner's needs and experiences without forsaking our own, our relationships become enriched with the play of complexity.

Your husband wants Chinese and you want baked chicken; and you've taken on the practice yes/and. What do you do? You say, "Okay. I've just started baking a chicken so why don't you swing by the restaurant and pick up some pot stickers and garlic spinach to go." You now don't have to prepare anything besides the chicken, your husband gets his Chinese food, and when you think about it, pot stickers and garlic spinach go perfectly with your grandma's baked chicken.

By practicing the skill of incorporation, of yes/and, we understand that the reality we come up with that validates all participants is a much more interesting one than what we might invent by rejecting our partner's offerings.

The Practice

Try out the practice of yes/and for an afternoon or a day or a week. Instead of saying no, catch yourself and say yes. Perhaps you have gone to see a movie with a friend. Your friend loved the movie and you loathed it. Rather than saying, "No, the movie was not profound and uplifting and you are an idiot for thinking there was even a single image to redeem that disgusting piece of trash," you might say, "Yes, when the woman sat down on the bed and removed her shoes, now that was a good scene," which is actually what you believe to be true. Then you can go on and criticize the lack of continuity and the bad editing with gusto. At which point your friend might respond, "Yes, I agree that the film was unrealistic and the editing klunky, and I also found it incredibly funny. I laughed really hard when the kid in shorts started dancing in the grocery store using the cereal boxes like maracas." And you remember that yes, that scene was in fact funny, and even though you are not in love with the film, you chuckle.

Without giving up your own point of view or sacrificing your own needs or ending up unbearably repressed, practice accepting all offerings. Yes/and instead of no/but.

"Let's go to yoga class."

"Yoga is fabulous and I love doing the downward dog and I was also thinking since it is such a beautiful day we might go to the beach. We could stretch on the sand."

This practice is surprisingly difficult, and part of what makes it amusing and profound is by taking it on for a day or a week or five minutes, we start to recognize the strange machinations of our minds; we see how we are stubborn and self-righteous and arbitrary in the ways that we clutch our opinions with a white-knuckled grip. As we let go of our beloved and hard-earned opinions about all and everything, we feel as though we are divesting ourselves of diver's weights and, slowly, we become buoyant.

Hospital Dancing

Last year, as I've mentioned, I underwent major surgery for a nebulous pre-cancerous condition. The suspicious cells turned out to be noninvasive, but the surgery entailed a major slice across my abdomen. The doctors urged me to walk as soon as possible so despite the fact that I could hardly manage to stand erect, let alone promenade, the nurses commanded me to march. Accompanied by my IV pole and a friend on each arm, I took a few agonizing steps down the hospital corridor. Within moments, I decided that if I had no choice but to silence the menacing nurses by being up and about, I might as well dance, which would most likely be considerably more healing than a somnambulant procession through antiseptic hallways. So between careful steps, I tossed a foot into the air, rocked my hips from side to side, and swayed my hands about. My friends, who were as eager as I was to enjoy hospital life as much as humanly possible, joined me.

An elderly man in a blue cotton gown that matched mine walked toward us with a friend on each of his elbows, which inspired my friends and me to dance with a bit more vim. Seeing us, the elderly man and his companions broke into a delicate fox-trot themselves. As we passed the hallway station, we swiveled our hips at the nurses and they, surprised but willing, swiveled back.

Patients waved to us from their open doorways as if we were the homecoming parade, and even a doctor rushing down the corridor with his stethoscope bouncing against his chest did a quick two-step.

While people may have thought us odd, they seemed to enjoy that we were dancing and because *we* were dancing, *they* could dance, as if we had been endowed with papal privileges and were bestowing dance consent to everyone we encountered.

My doctor made his rounds a few hours later.

"Have you walked yet?" he asked, leaning over me with a stern paternal right-in-the-eye gaze, his forehead knitted.

"No," I confessed.

"You have to . . ."

"I danced," I said, interrupting him before he could launch into his practiced spiel about how important postsurgical walking is even though you are crippled with pain, and lifting a foot a quarter-inch off the waxed linoleum floor requires the kind of courage only Olympic athletes cultivate. He looked puzzled, as if he didn't comprehend my words, and he was clearly unwilling to forego admonishment until I had obeyed his orders.

"I danced," I repeated more slowly and stared him in the eyes with the compassion of, say, Medusa.

Slowly, the meaning of my words registered, and he slapped my chart closed and headed for the door, pivoting on his toes like Fred Astaire as he turned to make his way down the hall.

Dancing helps us to heal from wounds of the body and soul. Dance whenever you can. Wherever you can. In the same way that astronauts plant flags on the moon and rock climbers plant flags on mountain peaks, plant dancing everywhere.

Giving

During my many years of studying Buddhism, I have heard a number of lectures on generosity, which is called *dana* in the Pali language. The most memorable were given by the venerable U Pandita, an esteemed Burmese master of Vipassana Buddhism. Unfamiliar with his reputation as being a rigorous meditation teacher who meted out a schedule beginning at four in the morning and continuing until eleven at night, divided into hour-long sessions alternating between sitting and walking while noting with precision the subtle movement of sensations, I enrolled in a two-week silent retreat.

Daily dharma talks provided the sole source of entertainment outside the myriad mind-states that tormented, delighted, or bored me as I sat and walked for hours, reining my attention to my body. I was, therefore, somewhat dismayed when U Pandita announced on the second day of the retreat that he would give his talk, again, on the topic he seemed to have covered in great detail the evening before. The famous meditation master spoke extremely slowly, in Burmese, and his translator spoke at an equally languid pace. I struggled to stay awake during the talk and to pay attention to this rare moment of receiving instruction from one of the world's great meditation masters, but my chin lurched toward my chest in uncontrollable spasms of fatigue.

On the third day, when U Pandita announced yet again that his talk would be on *dana,* disappointment moved in silent waves through the meditation hall of two hundred devotees sitting diligently on their cushions, longing for a moment of entertainment. I don't remember a single word U Pandita said. What I do remember is U Pandita's unflagging emphasis on the fact that generosity is the most fundamental of Buddhist practices and, until we understood its primary importance, he would not change the subject. Buddhism is not solely about sitting silently for weeks on end to achieve a concentrated state of mind that gives rise to insights. Buddhism, which teaches us that all beings are inextricably interconnected, is about generosity.

"Every time you have the urge to be generous, follow it," Jack Kornfield, another renowned Buddhist teacher, suggested during a dharma talk at Spirit Rock. The benefits of giving can be learned in the act of giving, he said, and suggested we take it on as a practice for a week. I followed Jack's advice and for a week, whenever the thought crossed my mind to give, I gave.

One afternoon, browsing in a chic houseware boutique in Berkeley, I spotted a yellow mug with a chartreuse chevron band that reminded me of my poet friend, Stefanie. Yellow and chartreuse are her favorite colors, and her most recent volume of poetry had featured a yellow and chartreuse jacket. I bought two mugs, which were on sale, one for Stefanie and one for me. When we met at the gym the next day for our evening workout, I pulled the gift out of my gear bag and handed it to her.

"Looks like you," I said.

She agreed and handed it back to me.

"It's a gift," I said, and a look of surprise flashed in Stefanie's eyes. A very brief moment passed before she understood I was actually giving her a present, even though it wasn't her birthday or Christmas. And then she broke into a big grin and thanked me, and I realized I was remarkably happy.

During the days of practicing and contemplating generosity, it began to dawn on me that giving is not only of value because of the pleasure the recipient enjoys, but giving is of value because of the pleasure the donor enjoys. Giving makes the giver happy. Giving opens the heart.

Often, we wait for events—birthdays, anniversaries, baby showers, weddings—to offer gifts to our friends. But the joy of giving doesn't need to be restricted to "appropriate" occasions. And we don't have to be rich.

Driving home from Big Sur shortly after the El Niño storms had passed, I found myself behind an old dented pickup truck. The roads had been badly damaged by mudslides and repair crews were at work day and night rebuilding the cliffside highway. Each time we passed a road crew, the driver of the old truck slowed to a stop and handed the workmen oranges. Each time, even though I was neither the giver nor the receiver but only the witness of this act, I felt the joy of the exchange. What could have been a tedious and unnerving drive home waiting repeatedly at lengthy roadblocks became joyful as I anticipated and witnessed the gift of oranges.

The ripples of generosity move out into the world in ways we might never know, but they move out as inevitably as ripples in a pool of water when even a tiny pebble is tossed. Our actions have effects; this is the law of dependent co-arising, one of the Buddha's greatest teachings. Because we have been kind, we create the conditions for another person to be kind.

What does generosity have to do with creativity? Inspiration is a gift. We say that artists who have a particular talent are gifted. We do not create inspiration, we receive inspiration. The very word "inspire" means to breathe in and inspiration is given as freely as our breath. To make any kind of art, we must be able to receive inspiration from our hearts, our minds, the spirits, the Creator and then give it form. This keeps the flow of inspiration moving without obstruction. This is the Dharma, the Way, the Tao.

The most subtle form of *dana* is having a mind that is generous, a heart that wishes well-being for ourselves and our friends and our colleagues, for all the beings of the world, all the beings of the universe, of all universes. Perhaps the greatest act of creative self-expression is to have a generous heart. And in the moment when the heart is opened with well-wishing, that is the moment when the impulse to sing arises, when the impulse to dance arises, when the impulse to write poetry arises, or to draw or paint or sculpt. It is in that moment that we have the opportunity to be generous, finally, to ourselves. It is in that moment that we have the opportunity to honor Creativity with our dancing and our singing as our prayers.

The Practice

If you run across something inexpensive that you know one of your friends might enjoy, go ahead, purchase it, and give it to your friend. Or perhaps you notice an item of clothing in your closet that you imagine a friend would appreciate. Give it away. Or a favorite ritual object. Or a blue stone with a white vein. Or a piece of fruit. Perhaps you might feel inspired to take your neighbor's dog for a walk. Or deliver a pot of soup to someone who is ill. Or give an acquaintance in a next-door office a flower. Follow your impulse. Don't hold back. Give.

We do not have to give away all of our possessions to enjoy the gift of giving. We can be simple. Modest. We can give surprise gifts. We can pay for the bridge toll of the car behind us, driven by a stranger. We can pick up the trash in the park.

We can also give an offering to someone we dislike as a way of softening our own hearts in an effort to arouse compassion for those we consider to be enemies.

On her way home from visiting her ailing mother recently, a friend of mine found a fresh lei of ginger blossoms and orchids looped around her car antenna in the airport parking lot. She was beaming when I saw her. The universe is magical without our help, but life is more fun when we make magic with her.

Generosity is not only the giving of things, but also the giving of warmth, affection, gratitude, appreciation, and humor. In the same way we can practice giving things to people, we can also practice giving compliments. We can tell a colleague that she looks particularly strik-ing in her red coat; we can tell the man at the bank how refreshing it is that he seems so relaxed and friendly; we can tell a neighbor that she has a lovely flower garden. We can give voice to what it is that we appreciate about one another.

We can also be generous in our actions: allowing a stranger to

move ahead of us when waiting for the ATM machine; or opening the
door for someone; or if a friend is in pain, giving her head or hands or
shoulders a brief massage. When we pay attention, we are moved
often during a day to express some form of giving, but we censor
those impulses. Perhaps we have gone too far in our attempts to let
one another lead private lives. Perhaps our gentle, sensitive, playful offerings will add moments of joy to our lives.

A Moment of Silence

*"All true artists, whether they know it or not, create from a place of no-mind,
from inner stillness. The mind then gives form to the creative impulse. Even
the great scientists have reported that their creative breakthroughs came at a
time of mental quietude."*

—ECKHART TOLLE

For years, I lived with a partner who was a producer. In the morning, a split
second after awakening, he would roll over in bed and grab the telephone. The
first call centered him in the world of business, the familiar challenges over-
riding any impulses that might be pulling him into the subterranean territory
of the still-waking mind, a place of chaos, yearning, unpredictability, and images. He was not a man who lacked creativity or dreams, and yet at the moment he awoke he was struck by a discomfort that he averted by grabbing the
telephone and orienting himself in a world that made sense.

I, too, grab the phone when I am feeling disoriented or uncomfortable. I
call a friend, or order something from a catalog, or check my messages, or return a business call rather than sink into the uneasiness and investigate my
inner experience.

To recapture our creativity, we need to muster the courage to linger in
the land of ambiguity, imagery, emotions, and intuition. We need to avert our

impulse to live only in the world of materialism, logic, and ambition, and listen to our inner beings.

Creativity arises from the ground of silence. Like clearing the yard of weeds and stones before planting seeds, silence clears the body and the mind so that creative impulses have an open field in which to emerge. The price we pay for being active in the modern world is that our minds are cluttered with to-do lists. These tasks captivate our attention and we lose access to our subconscious, the territory of creative self-expression.

I was at a retreat for artists several years ago that was conducted by Thich Nhat Hanh to examine the relationship between art, social activism, and Buddhist practice. The first morning, we gathered under the generous canopy of a hundred-year-old oak tree. Thây sat in front of us in his brown robes and was silent for several minutes. Finally, he spoke.

"Do nothing today. Be quiet. Tomorrow we will meet again."

A sigh of disappointment rippled through the crowd. We were activists, we wanted to receive teachings so we could get on with improving the world. But we had no choice, Thây was the teacher, and we followed his advice. The next morning we gathered again under the oak tree. Thây was silent for several minutes. Finally, he spoke.

"Do nothing today. Be quiet. Tomorrow we will gather in the morning."

An audible groan emerged from the crowd. We had given up ten days of our lives to receive teachings. Acres of rainforest were disappearing by the minute, hazardous waste was being dumped into rivers and streams, human rights were being violated in conflicts all over the world—we had vital work to do together. But again we surrendered to the guidance of our revered teacher.

I remember a moment of terror as I realized I had no idea of how I would spend the day—a looming expanse of uncharted space free of scheduled events, tasks to accomplish, plans. To my surprise, the hours unfolded seamlessly. I ate meals with new friends, took a hike in the woods, napped under a California bay laurel.

On the third morning, Thây was again silent. I felt him listening deeply to the mood of the crowd.

"Do nothing today," he said in a soft and even voice. "Be silent. Don't write in your journal and speak only when it is absolutely necessary."

A visceral anger bubbled up in the crowd. At least we could do formal meditation practice, we whispered to one another. But Thây forbade even that except for three half-hour sessions, one in the morning, one in the afternoon, and one in the evening.

Midmorning, I found myself perched on a hillside overlooking the golden rolling hills. The days of quiet had calmed me. I had no impulse to do anything aside from observing the patterns of grasses moving at the mercy of the wind. The choreography was complex and unpredictable. Delight struck me. The inner stillness I had cultivated had carved out the possibility for wonder.

The fourth morning when we gathered under the oak tree, Thây was again silent for several minutes. I could sense he was feeling the crowd, our inner rhythm, our capacity for calm.

"Today, we will begin a formal schedule," he said. "We will do meditation practice three times a day, walking meditation at eleven, and I will give a dharma talk at three. Now, you are ready."

———————————————

Creativity is fundamentally a matter of the mind synthesizing its inputs into outputs. But this is only a part of the truth. According to many sacred teachings and the revelations of quantum physics, if we look into the core of reality we catch a glimpse of emptiness. The ground of being is no ground; all reality arises from the void. Matter itself is made primarily of space. Yet we spend most of our lives avoiding this basic truth. We prefer to feel solid.

When an artist is poised on the brink of creation, she must come face-to-face with the void. Out of nothing, something will arise—but what? It is the blank page, the empty canvas, the vacant dance floor, the moment before speech, that is the most terrifying. And that is the moment so many of us turn away from and instead find some enticing chore like balancing our bank account or checking our e-mail to divert ourselves from the fear. To become

comfortable with creativity, we need to become comfortable with emptiness.

The following practices are deceptively simple. A myriad of reasons will
surface to avoid, delay, discount, critique, and minimize their importance:
"I'll do them later; I don't need *you* to tell me to do *that;* I am *so* familiar with
this practice from *so* many New Age self-help transform-your-life-in-ten-
easy-steps books I want to puke." But until we have the capacity to be still, to
be silent, until we have the discipline to listen to our innermost impulses,
until we have the facility to recognize the subconscious images that present
themselves to us, we cannot truly express our creative beings.

Most spiritual teachings are grounded in meditation practices that quiet
the mind. Many are complicated, many are simple. This is the simplest of all.

The Practice

You can do this practice anywhere: at your desk, on the beach, lying
down in bed, or riding the subway. You can do this practice anytime: in
the morning, in the middle of the workday, in the middle of the night.
You can do this practice alone, with a friend, with a group of friends,
sitting, standing, or lying down.

Find a comfortable position for your body that you can sustain
without moving for several minutes. Close your eyes. Be still. Feel the
breath come and go of its own volition, in its own rhythm. Feel where
the breath moves in the body: the diaphragm, the chest, the belly. Notice physical sensations—are you feeling pain anywhere, warmth or
coolness, tingling or tightness? Notice emotional sensations: sadness,
joy, anger, disappointment. Fall into the stillness. Do nothing. Notice
the thoughts that arise and pass away. Notice the sounds in the environment. Be quiet. When you are ready, after ten minutes, or five minutes, or one minute, open your eyes.

SKY GAZING

An alternate version of this exercise is the Tibetan Buddhist technique of sky gazing, which is done with the eyes open. Allow your gaze to be soft. Let the mind go soft and expansive like the sky, including and accepting everything that arises and passes away. As your gaze softens, allow your sense of self to soften as well, feeling the boundaries of your identity slip away. Dissolve into this sense of expansive being, being without borders, without end, luminous spacious being, for as long as you like.

Keeping the eyes open is a way to avert sleepiness, and to include vision as a component of meditation. We don't have to exclude any phenomena to experience an inner silence.

Hopefully you haven't written a poem or made up a song or redesigned your living room during your minutes of quiet, or perhaps you have and that is fine too, but not the point. So what does being silent for a few minutes have to do with creative freedom? By practicing stillness, we cultivate the courage to face the void. By practicing stillness, we touch the ground of being. Out of silence all creativity emerges.

Being quiet for even a minute has profound effects. If you are having a mental block at work, be quiet for a minute. If you are exhausted, be quiet for a minute. If you are on vacation, be quiet for a minute. Within a single moment of silence, freedom is born.

Freedom is our nature; freedom is the nature of our world. We may not consciously recognize an insight, a creative inspiration, a new way of seeing in the silence; we may not be able to identify the effect of the silence. It doesn't matter. By touching silence, we prepare the ground for all creative expression. By touching silence, we discover that the freedom we long for is at the heart of who we already are.

In the End

In the end, you are on your own. I can go on and on with practices and suggestions, but you are the one who must have fun. Throw yourself into it. Love making art. Hate making art. Kick and pout and moan while you make art. Make art when you feel like making art and when you don't feel like making art. Keep making art.

My nineteen-year-old nephew, Jonathon, is one of those kids who wears glasses and plays with computers around the clock. He was also inordinately shy, communicating primarily through monosyllables except when he conversed with his sister. Then he managed to speak in complete sentences, so I knew he had the capacity if not the inclination to do this. During these past two years at Stanford, Jonathon had taken only math and computer science classes. This summer, he decided to stay at school so his parents and I encouraged him to enrich his life and venture forth and try something new: sailing, or social dancing, or creative writing, or public speaking. Concerned for his psychological well-being since his grandfather had just died and days later his father had undergone heart surgery, I called him daily. I reached him in his dorm after the first day of classes and he informed me he had tried out an acting class.

"So, how was it?" I asked, imagining he would confess that he had stood on the sidelines and fled as soon as the teacher had offered the students a break.

"It was really FUN," Jonathon said, and he described in full sentences the theater games they had played.

When I called the next night, I asked what classes he had attended on his second day.

"I took another acting class," Jonathon said.

This time, I was the one who was speechless. He had planned to try out each of the classes, he said, and then enroll in the one he preferred.

"So what's the verdict?" I asked.

"I'm taking them both," he said.

Jonathon again described the exercises the teacher had offered, and he was talking now in paragraphs.

"It's amazing how quick the effect is," he said.

"And what's the effect?" I asked.

"I feel better," Jonathon said.

On the other end of the line, I raised my fist and punched the air and said, "Yes!"

"Wherever we may come alive, that is the area in which we are spiritual. To be vital, awake, aware, in all areas of our lives, is the task that is never accomplished, but it remains the goal."

—BROTHER DAVID STENDL-RAST

Acknowledgments

First and foremost, I would like to thank my students, who in their devotion to the craft of improvisation, have taught me how to teach, and in particular, Nina Jo Smith, who helped me craft the subtitle to this book. My performance partner, Corey Fischer, has been willing to experiment with me in the studio and on the stage for over a decade. Peter Barnes of Mesa Refuge, Bokara Legendre of the Medway Environmental Trust, Jan and Shawn Hailey and Susan Patner of the Gift House offered invaluable retreat time with gourmet meals and sweeping vistas. Esalen Institute has been another haven, where Michael Murphy and Nancy Lunney have provided me with the most exquisite of places to write, teach, and retreat, and the often beleaguered office staff (Mary Anne, Lois, Art, and Urgen) has graciously addressed my quirky needs. My writer friends, Natalie Goldberg, Wes Scoop Nisker, Jeff Greenwald, Susan Griffin, Dadie Donelly, and Stefanie Marlis, offered steady support and encouragement. Tano and Ayelet Maida entertained me with intelligent advice as I negotiated the new world of publishing. Hathaway Barry, Anne Cushman, and Annie Kunjappy provided insightful editorial comments, and Holly Hammond gave the manuscript a professional read—I am forever grateful for her sharp red pencil. My editor at Broadway, Lauren Marino, was a delightful collaborator and her suggestions helped to shape and hone the book. Rebecca Cole, also an editor at Broadway, handled the manuscript with delightful skill and enthusiasm. And

Gray Cutler, my copy editor, made precise, intelligent, and legible marks, which I cherished. My intrepid agent, Sarah Jane Freymann, worked above and beyond the call of duty as a nurse, a bed-and-breakfast hostess, and a caring confidante during times of travail, in addition to representing this book with ongoing fortitude and faith. And finally, I am indebted to my many spiritual teachers and friends, particularly H. W. L. Poonjaji, Ruth Denison, Thich Nhat Hanh, Tsoknyi Rimpoche, Zalman Schachter, Jack Kornfield, and Sylvia Boorstein, who over the years have directed me toward the often obscured light.

Bibliography and Sources

Adamson, Edward. *Art as Healing,* in association with John Timlin, foreword by Dr. Anthony Stevens. New York: Nicholas-Hays, Inc., 1984.

Ali, Hameed. Excerpt from a talk at Spirit Rock Meditation Center, Woodacre, California, May 2001.

Buechner, Frederick. Excerpt from essay by Frederick Buechner from *Spiritual Quest: The Art and Craft of Religious Writing,* introduction by William Zissner (Boston: Houghton Mifflin, 1988). I found this quote in Anne Lamott's wonderful book *Bird by Bird: Some Instructions on Writing and Life,* New York: Anchor Books/Doubleday, 1994.

Chaikin, Joseph. *The Presence of the Actor.* 1972. Reprint, New York: Theater Communications Group, 1991.

Davis, Avram, ed. *Meditation from the Heart of Judaism: Today's Teachers Share their Practices, Techniques and Faith.* Woodstock, Vt.: Jewish Lights Publications, 1997.

Dissanayake, Ellen. *Homo Aestheticus: Where Art Comes from and Why* (reprint). Seattle: University of Washington Press, 1995.

Eliot, T. S. *Four Quartets,* Harvest Books, 1974.

Linfante, Michele. "Remember," from *In the Direction of the Divine/Poems.* Forthcoming.

Mueller, Lisel. "Silence and Dancing," from *Alive Together: New and Selected Poems.* Baton Rouge and London: Louisiana State University Press, 1996.

Nachmanovitch, Stephen. *Free Play: The Power of Improvisation in Life and the Arts.* New York: A Jeremy P. Tarcher/Putnam book, 1990.

Paget, Lou. *How to Be a Great Lover: Girlfriend-to-Girlfriend Totally Explicit Techniques That Will Blow His Mind.* New York: Broadway Books, 1999.

Paley, Grace. *The Collected Stories.* New York: Farrar, Straus and Giroux, 1994.

Purce, Jill. Excerpt from a talk at the International Transpersonal Association conference, Santa Clara, California, 1995.

Rilke, Rainer Maria. *Letters to a Young Poet.* New York: Vintage Books, 1986.

Rossman, Dr. Martin. *Healing Yourself, A Step-by-Step Program for Better Health through Imagery.* New York: Walker, 1987.

Spolin, Viola. *Improvisation for the Theater: A Handbook of Teaching and Directing Techniques.* Chicago: Northwestern University Press, 1963.

Steindl-Rast, Brother David. *Gratefulness, the Heart of Prayer: An Approach to Life in Fullness.* New York: Paulist Press, 1984.

—: with Sharon Lebell and Kathleen Norris (introduction). *The Music of Silence: A Sacred Journey Through the Hours of the Day.* 2nd ed. Berkeley, Ca.: Seastone, 1998.

Tolle, Eckhart. *The Power of Now: A Guide to Spiritual Enlightenment.* Novato, Calif.: New World Library, 1999.

Underhill, Ruth Murray. *Singing for Power: The Song Magic of the Papago Indians of Southern Arizona;* foreword by Ofelia Zepeda. Tucson and London: The University of Arizona Press, 1938; 1966.

Index of Guidelines and Practices

six

Tea for Two

seven

When Gathered

eight

Enlivening Love

LUIS DELGADO

About the Author

Nina Wise graduated from UC Santa Cruz with a degree in
Religious Studies and the Aesthetics of Movement. She has devoted
her life to creating and performing in the world of experimental
theater and to investigating the relationship between art and spirit.
She has received three fellowships from the National Endowment
for the Arts among other honors. Nina leads workshops in her
unique form of improvisational being at the Motion Studio in San
Rafael, as well as at Esalen Institute and as an affiliate of Spirit Rock
Meditation Center.

For information on workshops and performances offered by Nina Wise, and a list of audio/video tapes of her work, please visit her website:

www.ninawise.com

or contact:
Motion Studio
124 Belvedere Street #7
San Rafael, CA 94901
(415) 459–3766
nina@ninawise.com